THE ART OF WAR

Strategic HR Applications for Today's Workforce

Sun Tzu
Tim Glowa
Lionel Giles
Forward by Suzanne Speak

Printed in the United States of America

ISBN: 9798328537452

Original text by Sun Tzu; translated into English by Lionel
Giles (1910); Interpreation for Human Resource (HR)
leaders by Tim Glowa; Foreword by Suzanne Speak

CONTENTS

To my dad, George

Your unwavering dedication, wisdom, and love have been my guiding light. Your life embodied the principles of resilience, integrity, and compassion, inspiring me every day. This book is a testament to the values you instilled in me and the countless lessons I learned from you.

Thank you for being my first and greatest teacher.

With all my love,
Tim Glowa

FOREWORD

Foreword

As the Vice President of Human Resources for a rapidly growing biotech research company, I have witnessed firsthand the profound impact of strategic HR leadership in fostering organizational success. In today's competitive landscape, the role of HR has evolved beyond administrative duties to become a cornerstone of strategic planning and execution. The wisdom of "Sun Tzu's The Art of War," a classic text that has guided leaders for centuries, offers invaluable insights that can be seamlessly applied to modern HR practices. This book, enhanced with HR applications by Tim Glowa, bridges ancient strategic principles with contemporary human resources management, providing a comprehensive guide for today's HR leaders.

Strategic Planning in HR

"Sun Tzu's The Art of War" is renowned for emphasizing strategic planning and foresight. In HR, strategic planning involves aligning human resources initiatives with the organization's goals. This alignment ensures that HR not only supports but also drives the achievement of business objectives. Tim Glowa's addition to this classic text provides HR professionals with practical applications of Sun Tzu's strategic principles, offering a roadmap for effective planning and execution.

One of the fundamental lessons from Sun Tzu is the

importance of thorough preparation and understanding of the environment. This lesson translates to a deep comprehension of the organizational landscape for HR leaders, including culture, workforce dynamics, and external market conditions. By leveraging this understanding, HR can develop strategies that anticipate and address potential challenges, ensuring the organization remains agile and resilient.

Leadership and Influence

Effective leadership is a core theme in Sun Tzu's teachings. The qualities of a successful leader—wisdom, sincerity, courage, and discipline—are critical for HR professionals tasked with guiding and influencing organizational culture and strategy. Tim Glowa's interpretations highlight how these timeless leadership qualities can be cultivated within the HR function.

HR leaders play a pivotal role in shaping the leadership pipeline within their organizations. By identifying and nurturing potential leaders, HR can ensure that the organization is equipped with individuals with the strategic acumen and ethical grounding necessary to lead effectively. The principles of Sun Tzu, when applied to HR, emphasize the importance of leading by example, maintaining integrity, and fostering a culture of continuous improvement.

Adaptability and Change Management

Sun Tzu's emphasis on adaptability and flexibility is particularly relevant in the fast-paced business world. The ability to pivot and adjust strategies in response to changing conditions is crucial for maintaining a competitive edge. For HR professionals, this means being proactive in managing change and ensuring that the organization can navigate transitions smoothly.

Tim Glowa's application of Sun Tzu's principles to

HR provides practical guidance on managing change effectively. This approach includes fostering a culture of resilience, encouraging innovation, and being prepared to adjust HR strategies in response to external and internal shifts. By embracing adaptability, HR leaders can help organizations thrive during constant change.

Building a Cohesive Organizational Culture

Sun Tzu's concept of the Moral Law underscores the importance of unity and alignment within an organization. For HR, this translates to building a solid and cohesive organizational culture where employees are aligned with the company's values and mission. A positive culture enhances employee engagement and retention and drives overall organizational performance.

Tim Glowa's insights provide HR professionals with strategies to cultivate and maintain a strong organizational culture. This perspective involves clear communication of values, consistently recognizing and rewarding employee contributions, and creating an inclusive and supportive work environment. By embedding these principles into their HR practices, leaders can foster a sense of belonging and purpose among employees, contributing to a more motivated and productive workforce.

Talent Management and Development:

Effective talent management is a critical component of HR's strategic role. Sun Tzu's teachings on understanding the strengths and weaknesses of one's forces offer valuable lessons for talent management. By leveraging data and analytics, HR professionals can gain insights into their workforce, identify skill gaps, and develop targeted recruitment, development, and retention strategies.

Tim Glowa's application of Sun Tzu's principles to talent management provides HR leaders with actionable strategies for optimizing their talent processes. This application includes aligning recruitment strategies with organizational goals, developing leadership capabilities within the HR team, and implementing robust performance management systems. By adopting a strategic approach to talent management, HR can ensure that the organization has the right people in the right roles, driving success and growth.

Conflict Resolution and Negotiation

Sun Tzu's expertise in strategy and tactics extends to conflict resolution and negotiation—areas where HR professionals often play a crucial role. Understanding the dynamics of conflict, anticipating the moves of opposing parties, and finding mutually beneficial solutions are skills that are as valuable in the corporate world as they are on the battlefield.

Tim Glowa's insights into Sun Tzu's strategies offer HR professionals practical tools for managing conflicts and negotiations within their organizations. HR leaders can create a more harmonious and collaborative work environment by promoting open communication, fostering empathy, and applying strategic thinking to conflict resolution. Additionally, practical negotiation skills can help HR navigate complex discussions and reach agreements that serve the best interests of both employees and the organization.

Embracing Technological Advancements

In an age where technology is transforming the workplace, HR leaders must be adept at integrating new tools and systems into their practices. Sun Tzu's emphasis on innovation and using all available resources aligns perfectly with the need for HR to embrace technological advancements.

Tim Glowa's interpretation includes the role of technology in modern HR practices, from AI-driven recruitment tools to advanced learning and development platforms. By leveraging technology, HR can enhance efficiency, improve decision-making, and provide a better employee experience. This forward-thinking approach is essential for HR leaders who want to stay ahead in a competitive landscape.

Conclusion: The Enduring Relevance of "Sun Tzu's Wisdom& The Art of War:

Strategic Insights for HR Leaders" is an invaluable resource for HR professionals seeking to elevate their strategic capabilities and drive organizational success. The timeless wisdom of Sun Tzu, combined with Tim Glowa's practical applications for HR, offers a comprehensive guide that is both insightful and actionable. This book underscores the importance of strategic planning, effective leadership, adaptability, and a solid organizational culture. It provides HR leaders with the tools and framework they need to navigate the complexities of their roles and make a meaningful impact on their organizations. As you embark on this journey through Sun Tzu's teachings and their application to HR, I encourage you to embrace these principles and let them guide you in pursuing excellence in human resources.

Suzanne Speak, MS-HRM, SHRM-SCP, SPHR

June 14, 2024

INTRODUCTION

"The Art of War" by Sun Tzu is more than just a military treatise; it is a timeless guide to strategy, leadership, and conflict resolution, offering profound insights that extend far beyond the battlefield. Written over two millennia ago, its teachings have influenced various aspects of modern life, including business, sports, personal development, and particularly Human Resources (HR). This book, featuring the original text of Sun Tzu's masterpiece, aims to bring its enduring wisdom to a new generation of HR professionals seeking insight and inspiration.

Imagine navigating the complexities of today's fast-paced corporate world with the clarity and precision of an ancient general. Sun Tzu's insights into human nature, strategic thinking, and effective decision-making provide a blueprint for overcoming challenges and achieving success in any organizational environment. Whether you are a leader in a corporate setting, an HR professional managing talent, or an individual striving for personal excellence, the principles outlined in this book will equip you with the tools to navigate and triumph in your professional battles.

One of the most captivating aspects of "The Art of War" is its applicability across various domains, including HR. Each chapter delves into different facets of strategy, from understanding the organizational landscape and knowing your workforce to the importance of flexibility and adaptation.

These timeless lessons are not confined to military strategy but extend to talent acquisition, employee engagement, conflict resolution, and change management. By studying Sun Tzu's approach to strategy, HR professionals can gain a competitive edge and cultivate a mindset geared toward success.

In the pages that follow, you will find the unaltered text of "The Art of War," presented with clarity and respect for its historical significance. Additionally, it will include an interpretation and explanation of the implications for HR leaders today, providing practical insights on how to apply Sun Tzu's timeless strategies to modern HR challenges. Tim Glowa's modern interpretation offers a fresh perspective, bridging the gap between ancient wisdom and contemporary HR practices.

As you immerse yourself in Sun Tzu's teachings, consider how these ancient strategies can be adapted to contemporary HR challenges. Reflect on the parallels between the art of war and the art of managing people and discover how timeless wisdom can illuminate your path to success in HR, whether you are negotiating with top talent, navigating organizational politics, or driving cultural transformation. From strategic planning and talent acquisition to leadership development and conflict resolution, the insights provided in this book will equip you with the tools to thrive in today's competitive corporate landscape.

Envision leading your HR team with the same strategic acumen as a battlefield general. Imagine being able to foresee and outmaneuver potential challenges, just as Sun Tzu advised in warfare. By understanding and implementing these strategies, you can foster a more resilient, adaptable, and motivated workforce. Whether it's through strategic planning that aligns with organizational goals, or by creating a culture that promotes engagement and retention, the lessons from "The Art of War" will enhance your ability to lead and inspire.

Embark on this journey through one of history's most influential works and unlock the secrets to mastering the art of HR strategy. Let "The Art of War" inspire and guide you, as it has done for countless leaders and thinkers throughout the ages. Prepare to see the corporate world through the eyes of a master strategist and equip yourself with the knowledge to conquer your greatest HR challenges. Dive into "The Art of War: Strategic Insights for HR Leaders" today and transform the way you manage and lead your organization, turning ancient wisdom into modern success.

Tim Glowa

Radium, British Columbia, Canada
June 13, 2024

THE ART OF WAR

Strategic HR Applications for Today's Workforce

SECTION 1

THE ART OF WAR

I. LAYING PLANS

1. Sun Tzu said: The art of war is of vital importance to the State.

2. It is a matter of life and death, a road either to safety or to ruin. Hence it is a subject of inquiry which can on no account be neglected.

3. The art of war, then, is governed by five constant factors, to be considered in one's deliberations, when seeking to determine the conditions obtaining in the field.

4. These are: (1) The Moral Law; (2) Heaven; (3) Earth; (4) The Commander; (5) Method and discipline.

5, 6. "The Moral Law" causes the people to be in complete accord with their ruler, so that they will follow him regardless of their lives, undismayed by any danger.

7. Heaven signifies night and day, cold and heat, times and seasons.

8. Earth comprises distances, great and small; danger and security; open ground and narrow passes; the chances of life and death.

9. The Commander stands for the virtues of wisdom, sincerity, benevolence, courage and strictness.

10. By "Method and discipline" are to be understood the marshalling of the army in its proper subdivisions, the gradations of rank among the officers, the maintenance of roads by which supplies may reach the army, and the control of military expenditure.

11. These five heads should be familiar to every general: he who knows them will be victorious; he who knows them not will fail.

12. Therefore, in your deliberations, when seeking to determine the military conditions, let them be made the basis of a comparison, in this wise: —

13. (1) Which of the two sovereigns is imbued with the Moral law? (2) Which of the two generals has most ability? (3) With whom lie the advantages derived from Heaven and Earth? (4) On which side is discipline most rigorously enforced? (5) Which army is the stronger? (6) On which side are officers and men more highly trained? (7) In which army is there the greater constancy both in reward and punishment?

14. By means of these seven considerations I can forecast victory or defeat.

15. The general that hearkens to my counsel and acts upon it, will conquer: let such a one be retained in command! The general that hearkens not to my counsel nor acts upon it, will suffer defeat: —let such a one be dismissed!

16. While heeding the profit of my counsel, avail yourself also of any helpful circumstances over and beyond the ordinary rules.

17. According as circumstances are favourable, one should modify one's plans.

18. All warfare is based on deception.

19. Hence, when able to attack, we must seem unable; when using our forces, we must seem inactive; when we are near, we must make the enemy believe we are far away; when far away, we must make him believe we are near.

20. Hold out baits to entice the enemy. Feign disorder and crush him.

21. If he is secure at all points, be prepared for him. If he is in

superior strength, evade him.

22. If your opponent is of choleric temper, seek to irritate him. Pretend to be weak, that he may grow arrogant.

23. If he is taking his ease, give him no rest. If his forces are united, separate them.

24. Attack him where he is unprepared, appear where you are not expected.

25. These military devices, leading to victory, must not be divulged beforehand.

26. Now the general who wins a battle makes many calculations in his temple ere the battle is fought. The general who loses a battle makes but few calculations beforehand. Thus do many calculations lead to victory, and few calculations to defeat how much more no calculation at all! It is by attention to this point that I can foresee who is likely to win or lose.

II. WAGING WAR

1. Sun Tzu said: In the operations of war, where there are in the field a thousand swift chariots, as many heavy chariots, and a hundred thousand mail-clad soldiers, with provisions enough to carry them a thousand "li" (A Li is a traditional Chinese unit of distance. Historically, the length of a li has varied, but it has been standardized in modern times. Today, one li is equivalent to exactly 500 meters, or half a kilometer. This unit is also sometimes referred to as the "Chinese mile."), the expenditure at home and at the front, including entertainment of guests, small items such as glue and paint, and sums spent on chariots and armour, will reach the total of a thousand ounces of silver per day. Such is the cost of raising an army of 100,000 men.

2. When you engage in actual fighting, if victory is long in coming, the men's weapons will grow dull, and their ardor will be damped. If you lay siege to a town, you will exhaust your strength.

3. Again, if the campaign is protracted, the resources of the State will not be equal to the strain.

4. Now, when your weapons are dulled, your ardour damped, your strength exhausted and your treasure spent, other chieftains will spring up to take advantage of your extremity. Then no man, however wise, will be able to avert the consequences that must ensue.

5. Thus, though we have heard of stupid haste in war, cleverness has never been seen associated with long delays.

6. There is no instance of a country having benefited from

prolonged warfare.

7. It is only one who is thoroughly acquainted with the evils of war that can thoroughly understand the profitable way of carrying it on.

8. The skillful soldier does not raise a second levy, neither are his supply-waggons loaded more than twice.

9. Bring war material with you from home, but forage on the enemy. Thus the army will have food enough for its needs.

10. Poverty of the State exchequer causes an army to be maintained by contributions from a distance. Contributing to maintain an army at a distance causes the people to be impoverished.

11. On the other hand, the proximity of an army causes prices to go up; and high prices cause the people's substance to be drained away.

12. When their substance is drained away, the peasantry will be afflicted by heavy exactions.

13, 14. With this loss of substance and exhaustion of strength, the homes of the people will be stripped bare, and three-tenths of their incomes will be dissipated; while Government expenses for broken chariots, worn-out horses, breastplates and helmets, bows and arrows, spears and shields, protective mantlets, draught-oxen and heavy wagons, will amount to four-tenths of its total revenue.

15. Hence a wise general makes a point of foraging on the enemy. One cartload of the enemy's provisions is equivalent to twenty of one's own, and likewise a single picul of his provender is equivalent to twenty from one's own store.

16. Now to kill the enemy, our men must be roused to anger; that there may be advantage from defeating the enemy, they must have their rewards.

17. Therefore, in chariot fighting, when ten or more chariots have been taken, those should be rewarded who took the first. Our own flags should be substituted for those of the enemy, and the chariots mingled and used in conjunction with ours. The captured soldiers should be kindly treated and kept.

18. This is called, using the conquered foe to augment one's own strength.

19. In war, then, let your great object be victory, not lengthy campaigns.

20. Thus, it may be known that the leader of armies is the arbiter of the people's fate, the man on whom it depends whether the nation shall be in peace or in peril.

III. ATTACK BY STRATAGEM

1. Sun Tzu said: In the practical art of war, the best thing of all is to take the enemy's country whole and intact; to shatter and destroy it is not so good. So, too, it is better to capture an army entire than to destroy it, to capture a regiment, a detachment or a company entire than to destroy them.

2. Hence to fight and conquer in all your battles is not supreme excellence; supreme excellence consists in breaking the enemy's resistance without fighting.

3. Thus, the highest form of generalship is to baulk the enemy's plans; the next best is to prevent the junction of the enemy's forces; the next in order is to attack the enemy's army in the field; and the worst policy of all is to besiege walled cities.

4. The rule is, not to besiege walled cities if it can possibly be avoided. The preparation of mantlets, movable shelters, and various implements of war, will take up three whole months; and the piling up of mounds over against the walls will take three months more.

5. The general, unable to control his irritation, will launch his men to the assault like swarming ants, with the result that one-third of his men are slain, while the town remains untaken. Such are the disastrous effects of a siege.

6. Therefore, the skillful leader subdues the enemy's troops without any fighting; he captures their cities without laying

siege to them; he overthrows their kingdom without lengthy operations in the field.

7. With his forces intact, he will dispute the mastery of the Empire, and thus, without losing a man, his triumph will be complete. This is the method of attacking by stratagem.

8. It is the rule in war, if our forces are ten to the enemy's one, to surround him; if five to one, to attack him; if twice as numerous, to divide our army into two.

9. If equally matched, we can offer battle; if slightly inferior in numbers, we can avoid the enemy; if quite unequal in every way, we can flee from him.

10. Hence, though an obstinate fight may be made by a small force, in the end it must be captured by the larger force.

11. Now the general is the bulwark of the State: if the bulwark is complete at all points; the State will be strong; if the bulwark is defective, the State will be weak.

12. There are three ways in which a ruler can bring misfortune upon his army: —

13. (1) By commanding the army to advance or to retreat, being ignorant of the fact that it cannot obey. This is called hobbling the army.

14. (2) By attempting to govern an army in the same way as he administers a kingdom, being ignorant of the conditions which obtain in an army. This causes restlessness in the soldier's minds.

15. (3) By employing the officers of his army without discrimination, through ignorance of the military principle of adaptation to circumstances. This shakes the confidence of the soldiers.

16. But when the army is restless and distrustful, trouble is sure to come from the other feudal princes. This is simply bringing

anarchy into the army and flinging victory away.

17. Thus, we may know that there are five essentials for victory: (1) He will win who knows when to fight and when not to fight. (2) He will win who knows how to handle both superior and inferior forces. (3) He will win whose army is animated by the same spirit throughout all its ranks. (4) He will win who, prepared himself, waits to take the enemy unprepared. (5) He will win who has military capacity and is not interfered with by the sovereign. Victory lies in the knowledge of these five points.

18. Hence the saying: If you know the enemy and know yourself, you need not fear the result of a hundred battles. If you know yourself but not the enemy, for every victory gained you will also suffer a defeat. If you know neither the enemy nor yourself, you will succumb in every battle.

IV. TACTICAL DISPOSITIONS

1. Sun Tzu said: The good fighters of old first put themselves beyond the possibility of defeat, and then waited for an opportunity of defeating the enemy.

2. To secure ourselves against defeat lies in our own hands, but the opportunity of defeating the enemy is provided by the enemy himself.

3. Thus, the good fighter is able to secure himself against defeat, but cannot make certain of defeating the enemy.

4. Hence the saying: One may "know" how to conquer without being able to "do" it.

5. Security against defeat implies defensive tactics; ability to defeat the enemy means taking the offensive.

6. Standing on the defensive indicates insufficient strength; attacking, a superabundance of strength.

7. The general who is skilled in defense hides in the most secret recesses of the earth; he who is skilled in attack flashes forth from the topmost heights of heaven. Thus, on the one hand we have ability to protect ourselves; on the other, a victory that is complete.

8. To see victory only when it is within the ken of the common herd is not the acme of excellence.

9. Neither is it the acme of excellence if you fight and conquer

and the whole Empire says, "Well done!"

10. To lift an autumn hair is no sign of great strength; to see sun and moon is no sign of sharp sight; to hear the noise of thunder is no sign of a quick ear.

11. What the ancients called a clever fighter is one who not only wins but excels in winning with ease.

12. Hence his victories bring him neither reputation for wisdom nor credit for courage.

13. He wins his battles by making no mistakes. Making no mistakes is what establishes the certainty of victory, for it means conquering an enemy that is already defeated.

14. Hence the skillful fighter puts himself into a position which makes defeat impossible and does not miss the moment for defeating the enemy.

15. Thus, it is that in war the victorious strategist only seeks battle after the victory has been won, whereas he who is destined to defeat first fights and afterwards looks for victory.

16. The consummate leader cultivates the moral law, and strictly adheres to method and discipline; thus, it is in his power to control success.

17. In respect of military method, we have, firstly, Measurement; secondly, Estimation of quantity; thirdly, Calculation; fourthly, Balancing of chances; fifthly, Victory.

18. Measurement owes its existence to Earth; Estimation of quantity to Measurement; Calculation to Estimation of quantity; Balancing of chances to Calculation; and Victory to Balancing of chances.

19. A victorious army opposed to a routed one, is as a pound's weight placed in the scale against a single grain.

20. The onrush of a conquering force is like the bursting of pent-

up waters into a chasm a thousand fathoms deep. So much for tactical dispositions.

V. ENERGY

1. Sun Tzu said: The control of a large force is the same principle as the control of a few men: it is merely a question of dividing up their numbers.

2. Fighting with a large army under your command is nowise different from fighting with a small one: it is merely a question of instituting signs and signals.

3. To ensure that your whole host may withstand the brunt of the enemy's attack and remain unshaken—this is affected by maneuvers direct and indirect.

4. That the impact of your army may be like a grindstone dashed against an egg—this is affected by the science of weak points and strong.

5. In all fighting, the direct method may be used for joining battle, but indirect methods will be needed to secure victory.

6. Indirect tactics, efficiently applied, are inexhaustible as Heaven and Earth, unending as the flow of rivers and streams; like the sun and moon, they end but to begin anew; like the four seasons, they pass away but to return once more.

7. There are not more than five musical notes, yet the combinations of these five give rise to more melodies than can ever be heard.

8. There are not more than five primary colours (blue, yellow, red, white, and black), yet in combination they produce more hues than can ever be seen.

9. There are not more than five cardinal tastes (sour, acrid, salt, sweet, bitter), yet combinations of them yield more flavors than can ever be tasted.

10. In battle, there are not more than two methods of attack—the direct and the indirect; yet these two in combination give rise to an endless series of maneuvers.

11. The direct and the indirect lead on to each other in turn. It is like moving in a circle—you never come to an end. Who can exhaust the possibilities of their combination?

12. The onset of troops is like the rush of a torrent which will even roll stones along in its course.

13. The quality of decision is like the well-timed swoop of a falcon which enables it to strike and destroy its victim.

14. Therefore, the good fighter will be terrible in his onset, and prompt in his decision.

15. Energy may be likened to the bending of a crossbow; decision, to the releasing of the trigger.

16. Amid the turmoil and tumult of battle, there may be seeming disorder and yet no real disorder at all; amid confusion and chaos, your array may be without head or tail, yet it will be proof against defeat.

17. Simulated disorder postulates perfect discipline; simulated fear postulates courage; simulated weakness postulates strength.

18. Hiding order beneath the cloak of disorder is simply a question of subdivision; concealing courage under a show of timidity presupposes a fund of latent energy; masking strength with weakness is to be affected by tactical dispositions.

19. Thus, one who is skillful at keeping the enemy on the move maintains deceitful appearances, according to which the enemy

will act. He sacrifices something, that the enemy may snatch at it.

20. By holding out baits, he keeps him on the march; then with a body of picked men he lies in wait for him.

21. The clever combatant looks to the effect of combined energy and does not require too much from individuals. Hence his ability to pick out the right men and utilize combined energy.

22. When he utilizes combined energy, his fighting men become as it were like unto rolling logs or stones. For it is the nature of a log or stone to remain motionless on level ground, and to move when on a slope; if four-cornered, to come to a standstill, but if round-shaped, to go rolling down.

23. Thus, the energy developed by good fighting men is as the momentum of a round stone rolled down a mountain thousands of feet in height. So much about energy.

VI. WEAK POINTS AND STRONG

1. Sun Tzu said: Whoever is first in the field and awaits the coming of the enemy, will be fresh for the fight; whoever is second in the field and must hasten to battle, will arrive exhausted.

2. Therefore, the clever combatant imposes his will on the enemy, but does not allow the enemy's will to be imposed on him.

3. By holding out advantages to him, he can cause the enemy to approach of his own accord; or, by inflicting damage, he can make it impossible for the enemy to draw near.

4. If the enemy is taking his ease, he can harass him; if well supplied with food, he can starve him out; if quietly encamped, he can force him to move.

5. Appear at points which the enemy must hasten to defend; march swiftly to places where you are not expected.

6. An army may march great distances without distress, if it marches through country where the enemy is not.

7. You can be sure of succeeding in your attacks if you only attack places which are undefended. You can ensure the safety of your defense if you only hold positions that cannot be attacked.

8. Hence that general is skillful in attack whose opponent does not know what to defend; and he is skillful in defense whose

opponent does not know what to attack.

9. O divine art of subtlety and secrecy! Through you we learn to be invisible, through you inaudible; and hence we can hold the enemy's fate in our hands.

10. You may advance and be irresistible, if you make for the enemy's weak points; you may retire and be safe from pursuit if your movements are more rapid than those of the enemy.

11. If we wish to fight, the enemy can be forced to an engagement even though he be sheltered behind a high rampart and a deep ditch. All we need do is attack some other place that he will be obliged to relieve.

12. If we do not wish to fight, we can prevent the enemy from engaging us even though the lines of our encampment be merely traced out on the ground. All we need do is to throw something odd and unaccountable in his way.

13. By discovering the enemy's dispositions and remaining invisible ourselves, we can keep our forces concentrated, while the enemy's must be divided.

14. We can form a single united body, while the enemy must split up into fractions. Hence there will be a whole pitted against separate parts of a whole, which means that we shall be many to the enemies few.

15. And if we are able thus to attack an inferior force with a superior one, our opponents will be in dire straits.

16. The spot where we intend to fight must not be made known; for then the enemy will have to prepare against a possible attack at several different points; and his forces being thus distributed in many directions, the numbers we shall have to face at any given point will be proportionately few.

17. For should the enemy strengthen his van, he will weaken his rear; should he strengthen his rear, he will weaken his van;

should he strengthen his left, he will weaken his right; should he strengthen his right, he will weaken his left. If he sends reinforcements everywhere, he will everywhere be weak.

18. Numerical weakness comes from having to prepare against possible attacks; numerical strength, from compelling our adversary to make these preparations against us.

19. Knowing the place and the time of the coming battle, we may concentrate from the greatest distances in order to fight.

20. But if neither time nor place be known, then the left wing will be impotent to succor the right, the right equally impotent to succor the left, the van unable to relieve the rear, or the rear to support the van. How much more so if the furthest portions of the army are anything under a hundred "li" apart, and even the nearest are separated by several "li"!

21. Though according to my estimate, the soldiers of Yueh exceed our own in number, that shall advantage them nothing in the matter of victory. I say then that victory can be achieved.

22. Though the enemy be stronger in numbers, we may prevent him from fighting. Scheme to discover his plans and the likelihood of their success.

23. Rouse him and learn the principle of his activity or inactivity. Force him to reveal himself, to find out his vulnerable spots.

24. Carefully compare the opposing army with your own, so that you may know where strength is superabundant and where it is deficient.

25. In making tactical dispositions, the highest pitch you can attain is to conceal them; conceal your dispositions, and you will be safe from the prying of the subtlest spies, from the machinations of the wisest brains.

26. How victory may be produced for them out of the enemy's own tactics—that is what the multitude cannot comprehend.

27. All men can see the tactics whereby I conquer, but what none can see is the strategy out of which victory has evolved.

28. Do not repeat the tactics which have gained you one victory, but let your methods be regulated by the infinite variety of circumstances.

29. Military tactics are like unto water; for water in its natural course runs away from high places and hastens downwards.

30. So, in war, the way is to avoid what is strong and to strike at what is weak.

31. Water shapes its course according to the nature of the ground over which it flows; the soldier works out his victory in relation to the foe whom he is facing.

32. Therefore, just as water retains no constant shape, so in warfare there are no constant conditions.

33. He who can modify his tactics in relation to his opponent and thereby succeed in winning, may be called a heaven-born captain.

34. The five elements (water, fire, wood, metal, earth) are not always equally predominant; the four seasons make way for each other in turn. There are short days and long; the moon has its periods of waning and waxing.

VII. MANEUVERING

1. Sun Tzu said: In war, the general receives his commands from the sovereign.

2. Having collected an army and concentrated his forces, he must blend and harmonize the different elements thereof before pitching his camp.

3. After that, comes tactical maneuvering, then which there is nothing more difficult. The difficulty of tactical maneuvering consists in turning the devious into the direct, and misfortune into gain.

4. Thus, to take a long and circuitous route, after enticing the enemy out of the way, and though starting after him, to contrive to reach the goal before him, shows knowledge of the artifice of "deviation".

5. Maneuvering with an army is advantageous; with an undisciplined multitude, most dangerous.

6. If you set a fully equipped army in march to snatch an advantage, the chances are that you will be too late. On the other hand, to detach a flying column for the purpose involves the sacrifice of its baggage and stores.

7. Thus, if you order your men to roll up their buff-coats, and make forced marches without halting day or night, covering double the usual distance at a stretch, doing a hundred "li" to wrest an advantage, the leaders of all your three divisions will fall into the hands of the enemy.

8. The stronger men will be in front, the jaded ones will fall

behind, and on this plan only one-tenth of your army will reach its destination.

9. If you march fifty "li" to outmaneuver the enemy, you will lose the leader of your first division, and only half your force will reach the goal.

10. If you march thirty "li" with the same object, two-thirds of your army will arrive.

11. We may take it then that an army without its baggage-train is lost; without provisions it is lost; without bases of supply, it is lost.

12. We cannot enter alliances until we are acquainted with the designs of our neighbors.

13. We are not fit to lead an army on the march unless we are familiar with the face of the country—its mountains and forests, its pitfalls and precipices, its marshes and swamps.

14. We shall be unable to turn natural advantages to account unless we make use of local guides.

15. In war, practice dissimulation, and you will succeed. Move only if there is a real advantage to be gained.

16. Whether to concentrate or to divide your troops, must be decided by circumstances.

17. Let your rapidity be that of the wind, your compactness that of the forest.

18. In raiding and plundering be like fire, in immovability like a mountain.

19. Let your plans be dark and impenetrable as night, and when you move, fall like a thunderbolt.

20. When you plunder a countryside, let the spoil be divided amongst your men; when you capture new territory, cut it up into allotments for the benefit of the soldiery.

21. Ponder and deliberate before you make a move.

22. He will conquer who has learnt the artifice of deviation. Such is the art of maneuvering.

23. The Book of Army Management says: On the field of battle, the spoken word does not carry far enough: hence the institution of gongs and drums. Nor can ordinary objects be seen clearly enough: hence the institution of banners and flags.

24. Gongs and drums, banners and flags, are means whereby the ears and eyes of the host may be focused on one point.

25. The host thus forming a single united body, is it impossible either for the brave to advance alone, or for the cowardly to retreat alone. This is the art of handling large masses of men.

26. In night-fighting, then, make much use of signal-fires and drums, and in fighting by day, of flags and banners, as a means of influencing the ears and eyes of your army.

27. A whole army may be robbed of its spirit; a commander-in-chief may be robbed of his presence of mind.

28. Now a soldier's spirit is keenest in the morning; by noonday it has begun to flag; and in the evening, his mind is bent only on returning to camp.

29. A clever general, therefore, avoids an army when its spirit is keen, but attacks it when it is sluggish and inclined to return. This is the art of studying moods.

30. Disciplined and calm, to await the appearance of disorder and hubbub amongst the enemy: —this is the art of retaining self-possession.

31. To be near the goal while the enemy is still far from it, to wait at ease while the enemy is toiling and struggling, to be well-fed while the enemy is famished: —this is the art of husbanding one's strength.

32. To refrain from intercepting an enemy whose banners are in perfect order, to refrain from attacking an army drawn up in calm and confident array: —this is the art of studying circumstances.

33. It is a military axiom not to advance uphill against the enemy, nor to oppose him when he comes downhill.

34. Do not pursue an enemy who simulates flight; do not attack soldiers whose temper is keen.

35. Do not swallow a bait offered by the enemy. Do not interfere with an army that is returning home.

36. When you surround an army, leave an outlet free. Do not press a desperate foe too hard.

37. Such is the art of warfare.

VIII. VARIATION
OF TACTICS

1. Sun Tzu said: In war, the general receives his commands from the sovereign, collects his army and concentrates his forces.

2. When in difficult country, do not encamp. In country where high roads intersect, join hands with your allies. Do not linger in dangerously isolated positions. In hemmed-in situations, you must resort to stratagem. In a desperate position, you must fight.

3. There are roads which must not be followed, armies which must be not attacked, towns which must not be besieged, positions which must not be contested, commands of the sovereign which must not be obeyed.

4. The general who thoroughly understands the advantages that accompany variation of tactics knows how to handle his troops.

5. The general who does not understand these, may be well acquainted with the configuration of the country, yet he will not be able to turn his knowledge to practical account.

6. So, the student of war who is unversed in the art of war of varying his plans, even though he be acquainted with the Five Advantages, will fail to make the best use of his men.

7. Hence in the wise leader's plans, considerations of advantage and of disadvantage will be blended.

8. If our expectation of advantage be tempered in this way, we

may succeed in accomplishing the essential part of our schemes.

9. If, on the other hand, during difficulties we are always ready to seize an advantage, we may extricate ourselves from misfortune.

10. Reduce the hostile chiefs by inflicting damage on them; and make trouble for them and keep them constantly engaged; hold out specious allurements and make them rush to any given point.

11. The art of war teaches us to rely not on the likelihood of the enemy's not coming, but on our own readiness to receive him; not on the chance of his not attacking, but rather on the fact that we have made our position unassailable.

12. There are five dangerous faults which may affect a general: (1) Recklessness, which leads to destruction; (2) cowardice, which leads to capture; (3) a hasty temper, which can be provoked by insults; (4) a delicacy of honor which is sensitive to shame; (5) over-solicitude for his men, which exposes him to worry and trouble.

13. These are the five besetting sins of a general, ruinous to the conduct of war.

14. When an army is overthrown and its leader slain, the cause will surely be found among these five dangerous faults. Let them be a subject of meditation.

IX. THE ARMY ON THE MARCH

1. Sun Tzu said: We come now to the question of encamping the army and observing signs of the enemy. Pass quickly over mountains and keep in the valleys.

2. Camp in high places, facing the sun. Do not climb heights to fight. So much for mountain warfare.

3. After crossing a river, you should get far away from it.

4. When an invading force crosses a river in its onward march, do not advance to meet it in mid-stream. It will be best to let half the army get across, and then deliver your attack.

5. If you are anxious to fight, you should not go to meet the invader near a river which he has to cross.

6. Moor your craft higher up than the enemy and facing the sun. Do not move up-stream to meet the enemy. So much for river warfare.

7. In crossing saltmarshes, your sole concern should be to get over them quickly, without any delay.

8. If forced to fight in a saltmarsh, you should have water and grass near you, and get your back to a clump of trees. So much for operations in saltmarshes.

9. In dry, level country, take up an easily accessible position with rising ground to your right and on your rear, so that the danger may be in front, and safety lie behind. So much for campaigning

in flat country.

10. These are the four useful branches of military knowledge which enabled the Yellow Emperor to vanquish four several sovereigns.

11. All armies prefer high ground to low, and sunny places to dark.

12. If you are careful of your men, and camp on hard ground, the army will be free from disease of every kind, and this will spell victory.

13. When you come to a hill or a bank, occupy the sunny side, with the slope on your right rear. Thus, you will at once act for the benefit of your soldiers and utilize the natural advantages of the ground.

14. When, in consequence of heavy rains up-country, a river which you wish to ford is swollen and flecked with foam, you must wait until it subsides.

15. Country in which there are precipitous cliffs with torrents running between, deep natural hollows, confined places, tangled thickets, quagmires and crevasses, should be left with all possible speed and not approached.

16. While we keep away from such places, we should get the enemy to approach them; while we face them, we should let the enemy have them on his rear.

17. If about your camp there should be any hilly country, ponds surrounded by aquatic grass, hollow basins filled with reeds, or woods with thick undergrowth, they must be carefully routed out and searched; for these are places where men in ambush or insidious spies are likely to be lurking.

18. When the enemy is close at hand and remains quiet, he is relying on the natural strength of his position.

19. When he keeps aloof and tries to provoke a battle, he is

anxious for the other side to advance.

20. If his place of encampment is easy of access, he is tendering a bait.

21. Movement amongst the trees of a forest shows that the enemy is advancing. The appearance of several screens amid thick grass means that the enemy wants to make us suspicious.

22. The rising of birds in their flight is the sign of an ambuscade. Startled beasts indicate that a sudden attack is coming.

23. When there is dust rising in a high column, it is the sign of chariots advancing; when the dust is low, but spread over a wide area, it betokens the approach of infantry. When it branches out in different directions, it shows that parties have been sent to collect firewood. A few clouds of dust moving to and from signify that the army is encamping.

24. Humble words and increased preparations are signs that the enemy is about to advance. Violent language and driving forward as if to the attack are signs that he will retreat.

25. When the light chariots come out first and take up a position on the wings, it is a sign that the enemy is forming for battle.

26. Peace proposals unaccompanied by a sworn covenant indicate a plot.

27. When there is much running about and the soldiers fall into rank, it means that the critical moment has come.

28. When some are seen advancing and some retreating, it is a lure.

29. When the soldiers stand leaning on their spears, they are faint from want of food.

30. If those who are sent to draw water begin by drinking themselves, the army is suffering from thirst.

31. If the enemy sees an advantage to be gained and makes no

effort to secure it, the soldiers are exhausted.

32. If birds gather on any spot, it is unoccupied. Clamor by night betokens nervousness.

33. If there is disturbance in the camp, the general's authority is weak. If the banners and flags are shifted about, sedition is afoot. If the officers are angry, it means that the men are weary.

34. When an army feeds its horses with grain and kills its cattle for food, and when the men do not hang their cooking-pots over the campfires, showing that they will not return to their tents, you may know that they are determined to fight to the death.

35. The sight of men whispering together in small knots or speaking in subdued tones points to disaffection amongst the rank and file.

36. Too frequent rewards signify that the enemy is at the end of his resources; too many punishments betray a condition of dire distress.

37. To begin by bluster, but afterwards to take fright at the enemy's numbers, shows a supreme lack of intelligence.

38. When envoys are sent with compliments in their mouths, it is a sign that the enemy wishes for a truce.

39. If the enemy's troops march up angrily and remain facing ours for a long time without either joining battle or taking themselves off again, the situation is one that demands great vigilance and circumspection.

40. If our troops are no more in number than the enemy, that is amply sufficient; it only means that no direct attack can be made. What we can do is simply to concentrate all our available strength, keep a close watch on the enemy, and obtain reinforcements.

41. He who exercises no forethought but makes light of his opponents is sure to be captured by them.

42. If soldiers are punished before they have grown attached to you, they will not prove submissive; and, unless submissive, then will be practically useless. If, when the soldiers have become attached to you, punishments are not enforced, they will still be useless.

43. Therefore, soldiers must be treated in the first instance with humanity but kept under control by means of iron discipline. This is a certain road to victory.

44. If in training soldiers' commands are habitually enforced, the army will be well-disciplined; if not, its discipline will be bad.

45. If a general shows confidence in his men but always insists on his orders being obeyed, the gain will be mutual.

X. TERRAIN

1. Sun Tzu said: We may distinguish six kinds of terrain, to wit: (1) Accessible ground; (2) entangling ground; (3) temporizing ground; (4) narrow passes; (5) precipitous heights; (6) positions at a great distance from the enemy.

2. Ground which can be freely traversed by both sides is called "accessible".

3. Regarding ground of this nature, be before the enemy in occupying the raised and sunny spots, and carefully guard your line of supplies. Then you will be able to fight with advantage.

4. Ground which can be abandoned but is hard to re-occupy is called "entangling".

5. From a position of this sort, if the enemy is unprepared, you may sally forth and defeat him. But if the enemy is prepared for your coming, and you fail to defeat him, then, return being impossible, disaster will ensue.

6. When the position is such that neither side will gain by making the first move, it is called temporizing ground.

7. In a position of this sort, even though the enemy should offer us an attractive bait, it will be advisable not to stir forth, but rather to retreat, thus enticing the enemy in his turn; then, when part of his army has come out, we may deliver our attack with advantage.

8. Regarding "narrow passes", if you can occupy them first, let them be strongly garrisoned and await the advent of the enemy.

9. Should the enemy forestall you in occupying a pass, do not go after him if the pass is fully garrisoned, but only if it is weakly garrisoned.

10. Regarding "precipitous heights", if you are beforehand with your adversary, you should occupy the raised and sunny spots, and there wait for him to come up.

11. If the enemy has occupied them before you, do not follow him, but retreat and try to entice him away.

12. If you are situated at a great distance from the enemy, and the strength of the two armies is equal, it is not easy to provoke a battle, and fighting will be to your disadvantage

13. These six are the principles connected with Earth. The general who has attained a responsible post must be careful to study them.

14. Now an army is exposed to six several calamities, not arising from natural causes, but from faults for which the general is responsible. These are: (1) Flight; (2) insubordination; (3) collapse; (4) ruin; (5) disorganization; (6) rout.

15. Other conditions being equal, if one force is hurled against another ten times its size, the result will be the "flight" of the former.

16. When the common soldiers are too strong and their officers too weak, the result is "insubordination". When the officers are too strong and the common soldiers too weak, the result is "collapse".

17. When the higher officers are angry and insubordinate, and on meeting the enemy give battle on their own account from a feeling of resentment, before the commander-in-chief can tell whether or not he is in a position to fight, the result is "ruin".

18. When the general is weak and without authority; when his orders are not clear and distinct; when there are no

fixed duties assigned to officers and men, and the ranks are formed in a slovenly haphazard manner, the result is utter "disorganization".

19. When a general, unable to estimate the enemy's strength, allows an inferior force to engage a larger one, or hurls a weak detachment against a powerful one, and neglects to place picked soldiers in the front rank, the result must be a "rout"

20. These are six ways of courting defeat, which must be carefully noted by the general who has attained a responsible post.

21. The natural formation of the country is the soldier's best ally; but a power of estimating the adversary, of controlling the forces of victory, and of shrewdly calculating difficulties, dangers and distances, constitutes the test of a great general.

22. He who knows these things, and in fighting puts his knowledge into practice, will win his battles. He who knows them not, nor practices them, will surely be defeated.

23. If fighting is sure to result in victory, then you must fight, even though the ruler forbids it; if fighting will not result in victory, then you must not fight even at the ruler's bidding.

24. The general who advances without coveting fame and retreats without fearing disgrace, whose only thought is to protect his country and do good service for his sovereign, is the jewel of the kingdom.

25. Regard your soldiers as your children, and they will follow you into the deepest valleys; look on them as your own beloved sons, and they will stand by you even unto death.

26. If, however, you are indulgent, but unable to make your authority felt; kind-hearted, but unable to enforce your commands; and incapable, moreover, of quelling disorder: then your soldiers must be likened to spoilt children; they are useless for any practical purpose.

27. If we know that our own men are in a condition to attack but are unaware that the enemy is not open to attack, we have gone only halfway towards victory.

28. If we know that the enemy is open to attack but are unaware that our own men are not in a condition to attack, we have gone only halfway towards victory.

29. If we know that the enemy is open to attack, and know that our men are in a condition to attack but are unaware that the nature of the ground makes fighting impracticable, we have still gone only halfway towards victory.

30. Hence the experienced soldier, once in motion, is never bewildered; once he has broken camp, he is never at a loss.

31. Hence the saying: If you know the enemy and know yourself, your victory will not stand in doubt; if you know Heaven and know Earth, you may make your victory complete.

XI. THE NINE SITUATIONS

1. Sun Tzu said: The art of war recognizes nine varieties of ground: (1) Dispersive ground; (2) facile ground; (3) contentious ground; (4) open ground; (5) ground of intersecting highways; (6) serious ground; (7) difficult ground; (8) hemmed-in ground; (9) desperate ground.

2. When a chieftain is fighting in his own territory, it is dispersive ground.

3. When he has penetrated hostile territory, but to no great distance, it is facile ground.

4. Ground the possession of which imports great advantage to either side, is contentious ground.

5. Ground on which each side has liberty of movement is open ground.

6. Ground which forms the key to three contiguous states, so that he who occupies it first has most of the Empire at his command, is ground of intersecting highways.

7. When an army has penetrated the heart of a hostile country, leaving a number of fortified cities in its rear, it is serious ground.

8. Mountain forests, rugged steeps, marshes and fens—all country that is hard to traverse: this is difficult ground.

9. Ground which is reached through narrow gorges, and from

which we can only retire by tortuous paths, so that a small number of the enemy would suffice to crush a large body of our men: this is hemmed in ground.

10. Ground on which we can only be saved from destruction by fighting without delay, is desperate ground.

11. On dispersive ground, therefore, fight not. On facile ground, halt not. On contentious ground, attack not.

12. On open ground, do not try to block the enemy's way. On ground of intersecting highways, join hands with your allies.

13. On serious ground, gather in plunder. In difficult ground, keep steadily on the march.

14. On hemmed-in ground, resort to stratagem. On desperate ground, fight.

15. Those who were called skillful leaders of old knew how to drive a wedge between the enemy's front and rear; to prevent co-operation between his large and small divisions; to hinder the good troops from rescuing the bad, the officers from rallying their men.

16. When the enemy's men were scattered, they prevented them from concentrating; even when their forces were united, they managed to keep them in disorder.

17. When it was to their advantage, they made a forward move; when otherwise, they stopped still.

18. If asked how to cope with a great host of the enemy in orderly array and on the point of marching to the attack, I should say: "Begin by seizing something which your opponent holds dear; then he will be amenable to your will."

19. Rapidity is the essence of war: take advantage of the enemy's unreadiness, make your way by unexpected routes, and attack unguarded spots.

20. The following are the principles to be observed by an invading force: The further you penetrate a country, the greater will be the solidarity of your troops, and thus the defenders will not prevail against you.

21. Make forays in fertile country to supply your army with food.

22. Carefully study the well-being of your men, and do not overtax them. Concentrate your energy and hoard your strength. Keep your army continually on the move and devise unfathomable plans.

23. Throw your soldiers into positions whence there is no escape, and they will prefer death to flight. If they will face death, there is nothing they may not achieve. Officers and men alike will put forth their uttermost strength.

24. Soldiers when in desperate straits lose the sense of fear. If there is no place of refuge, they will stand firm. If they are in the heart of a hostile country, they will show a stubborn front. If there is no help for it, they will fight hard.

25. Thus, without waiting to be marshalled, the soldiers will be constantly on the "qui vive"; without waiting to be asked, they will do your will; without restrictions, they will be faithful; without giving orders, they can be trusted.

26. Prohibit the taking of omens and do away with superstitious doubts. Then, until death itself comes, no calamity need be feared.

27. If our soldiers are not overburdened with money, it is not because they have a distaste for riches; if their lives are not unduly long, it is not because they are disinclined to longevity.

28. On the day they are ordered out to battle, your soldiers may weep, those sitting up bedewing their garments, and those lying down letting the tears run down their cheeks. But let them once be brought to bay, and they will display the courage of a Chu or a

Kuei.

29. The skillful tactician may be likened to the "shuai-jan" (sudden or rapid). Now the shuai-jan is a snake that is found in the Ch 'ang mountains. Strike at its head, and you will be attacked by its tail; strike at its tail, and you will be attacked by its head; strike at its middle, and you will be attacked by head and tail both.

30. Asked if an army can be made to imitate the "shuai-jan", I should answer, yes. For the men of Wu and the men of Yueh are enemies; yet if they are crossing a river in the same boat and are caught by a storm, they will come to each other's assistance just as the left hand helps the right.

31. Hence it is not enough to put one's trust in the tethering of horses, and the burying of chariot wheels in the ground.

32. The principle on which to manage an army is to set up one standard of courage which all must reach.33. How to make the best of both strong and weak—that is a question involving the proper use of ground.

34. Thus, the skillful general conducts his army just as though he were leading a single man, willy-nilly, by the hand.

35. It is the business of a general to be quiet and thus ensure secrecy; upright and just, and thus maintain order.

36. He must be able to mystify his officers and men by false reports and appearances, and thus keep them in total ignorance.

37. By altering his arrangements and changing his plans, he keeps the enemy without definite knowledge. By shifting his camp and taking circuitous routes, he prevents the enemy from anticipating his purpose.

38. At the critical moment, the leader of an army acts like one who has climbed up a height and then kicks away the ladder behind him. He carries his men deep into hostile territory before

he shows his hand.

39. He burns his boats and breaks his cooking-pots; like a shepherd driving a flock of sheep, he drives his men this way and that, and none knows whither he is going.

40. To muster his host and bring it into danger: —this may be termed the business of the general.

41. The different measures suited to the nine varieties of ground; the expediency of aggressive or defensive tactics; and the fundamental laws of human nature: these are things that must most certainly be studied.

42. When invading hostile territory, the general principle is, that penetrating deeply brings cohesion; penetrating but a short way means dispersion.

43. When you leave your own country behind, and take your army across neighborhood territory, you find yourself on critical ground. When there are means of communication on all four sides, the ground is one of intersecting highways.

44. When you penetrate deeply into a country, it is serious ground. When you penetrate but a little way, it is facile ground.

45. When you have the enemy's strongholds on your rear, and narrow passes in front, it is hemmed-in ground. When there is no place of refuge at all, it is desperate ground.

46. Therefore, on dispersive ground, I would inspire my men with unity of purpose. On facile ground, I would see that there is close connection between all parts of my army.

47. On contentious ground, I would hurry up my rear.

48. On open ground, I would keep a vigilant eye on my defenses. On ground of intersecting highways, I would consolidate my alliances.

49. On serious ground, I would try to ensure a continuous

stream of supplies. On difficult ground, I would keep pushing on along the road.

50. On hemmed-in ground, I would block any way of retreat. On desperate ground, I would proclaim to my soldiers the hopelessness of saving their lives.

51. For it is the soldier's disposition to offer an obstinate resistance when surrounded, to fight hard when he cannot help himself, and to obey promptly when he has fallen into danger.

52. We cannot enter alliance with neighboring princes until we are acquainted with their designs. We are not fit to lead an army on the march unless we are familiar with the face of the country—its mountains and forests, its pitfalls and precipices, its marshes and swamps. We shall be unable to turn natural advantages to account unless we make use of local guides.

53. To be ignorant of any one of the following four or five principles does not befit a warlike prince.

54. When a warlike prince attacks a powerful state, his generalship shows itself in preventing the concentration of the enemy's forces. He overawes his opponents, and their allies are prevented from joining against him.

55. Hence, he does not strive to ally himself with all and sundry, nor does he foster the power of other states. He carries out his own secret designs, keeping his antagonists in awe. Thus, he is able to capture their cities and overthrow their kingdoms.

56. Bestow rewards without regard to rule, issue orders without regard to previous arrangements; and you will be able to handle a whole army as though you had to do with but a single man.

57. Confront your soldiers with the deed itself; never let them know your design. When the outlook is bright, bring it before their eyes; but tell them nothing when the situation is gloomy.

58. Place your army in deadly peril, and it will survive; plunge it

into desperate straits, and it will come off in safety.

59. For it is precisely when a force has fallen into harm's way that can strike a blow for victory.

60. Success in warfare is gained by carefully accommodating ourselves to the enemy's purpose.

61. By persistently hanging on the enemy's flank, we shall succeed in the long run in killing the commander-in-chief.

62. This is called ability to accomplish a thing by sheer cunning.

63. On the day that you take up your command, block the frontier passes, destroy the official tallies, and stop the passage of all emissaries.

64. Be stern in the council-chamber, so that you may control the situation.

65. If the enemy leaves a door open, you must rush in.

66. Forestall your opponent by seizing what he holds dear, and subtly contrive to time his arrival on the ground.

67. Walk in the path defined by rule and accommodate yourself to the enemy until you can fight a decisive battle.

68. At first, then, exhibit the coyness of a maiden, until the enemy gives you an opening; afterwards emulate the rapidity of a running hare, and it will be too late for the enemy to oppose you.

XII. THE ATTACK
BY FIRE

1. Sun Tzu said: There are five ways of attacking with fire. The first is to burn soldiers in their camp; the second is to burn stores; the third is to burn baggage-trains; the fourth is to burn arsenals and magazines; the fifth is to hurl dropping fire amongst the enemy.

2. To carry out an attack, we must have means available. The material for raising fire should always be kept in readiness.

3. There is a proper season for making attacks with fire, and special days for starting a conflagration.

4. The proper season is when the weather is very dry; the special days are those when the moon is in the constellations of the Sieve, the Wall, the Wing or the Crossbar; for these four are all days of rising wind.

5. In attacking with fire, one should be prepared to meet five possible developments:

6. (1) When fire breaks out inside the enemy's camp, respond at once with an attack from without.

7. (2) If there is an outbreak of fire, but the enemy's soldiers remain quiet, bide your time and do not attack.

8. (3) When the force of the flames has reached its height, follow it up with an attack, if that is practicable; if not, stay where you are.

9. (4) If it is possible to make an assault with fire from without, do not wait for it to break out within, but deliver your attack at a favorable moment.

10. (5) When you start a fire, be to windward of it. Do not attack from the protected side.

11. A wind that rises in the daytime lasts long, but a night breeze soon falls.

12. In every army, the five developments connected with fire must be known, the movements of the stars calculated, and a watch kept for the proper days.

13. Hence those who use fire as an aid to the attack show intelligence; those who use water as an aid to the attack gain an accession of strength.

14. By means of water, an enemy may be intercepted, but not robbed of all his belongings.

15. Unhappy is the fate of one who tries to win his battles and succeed in his attacks without cultivating the spirit of enterprise; for the result is waste of time and general stagnation.

16. Hence the saying: The enlightened ruler lays his plans well ahead; the good general cultivates his resources.

17. Move not unless you see an advantage; use not your troops unless there is something to be gained; fight not unless the position is critical.

18. No ruler should put troops into the field merely to gratify his own spleen; no general should fight a battle simply out of pique.

19. If it is to your advantage, make a forward move; if not, stay where you are.

20. Anger may in time change to gladness; vexation may be succeeded by content.

21. But a kingdom that has once been destroyed can never come again into being nor can the dead ever be brought back to life.

22. Hence the enlightened ruler is heedful, and the good general full of caution. This is the way to keep a country at peace and an army intact.

XIII. THE USE OF SPIES

1. Sun Tzu said: Raising a host of a hundred thousand men and marching them great distances entails heavy loss on the people and a drain on the resources of the State. The daily expenditure will amount to a thousand ounces of silver. There will be commotion at home and abroad, and men will drop down exhausted on the highways. As many as seven hundred thousand families will be impeded in their labor.

2. Hostile armies may face each other for years, striving for the victory which is decided in a single day. This being so, to remain in ignorance of the enemy's condition simply because one grudges the outlay of a hundred ounces of silver in honours and emoluments, is the height of inhumanity.

3. One who acts thus is no leader of men, no present help to his sovereign, no master of victory.

4. Thus, what enables the wise sovereign and the good general to strike and conquer, and achieve things beyond the reach of ordinary men, is "foreknowledge".

5. Now this foreknowledge cannot be elicited from spirits; it cannot be obtained inductively from experience, nor by any deductive calculation.

6. Knowledge of the enemy's dispositions can only be obtained from other men.

7. Hence the use of spies, of whom there are five classes: (1) Local spies; (2) inward spies; (3) converted spies; (4) doomed spies; (5) surviving spies.

8. When these five kinds of spy are all at work, none can discover the secret system. This is called "divine manipulation of the threads." It is the sovereign's most precious faculty.

9. Having "local spies" means employing the services of the inhabitants of a district.

10. Having "inward spies", making use of officials of the enemy.

11. Having "converted spies", getting hold of the enemy's spies and using them for our own purposes.

12. Having "doomed spies", doing certain things openly for purposes of deception, and allowing our own spies to know of them and report them to the enemy.

13. "Surviving spies", finally, are those who bring back news from the enemy's camp.

14. Hence it is that with none in the whole army are more intimate relations to be maintained than with spies. None should be more liberally rewarded. In no other business should greater secrecy be preserved.

15. Spies cannot be usefully employed without a certain intuitive sagacity.

16. They cannot be properly managed without benevolence and straightforwardness.

17. Without subtle ingenuity of mind, one cannot make certain of the truth of their reports.

18. Be subtle! be subtle! and use your spies for every kind of business.

19. If a secret piece of news is divulged by a spy before the time is ripe, he must be put to death together with the man to whom the secret was told.

20. Whether the object be to crush an army, to storm a city, or

to assassinate an individual, it is always necessary to begin by finding out the names of the attendants, the aides-de-camp, the doorkeepers and sentries of the general in command. Our spies must be commissioned to ascertain these.

21. The enemy's spies who have come to spy on us must be sought out, tempted with bribes, led away and comfortably housed. Thus, they will become converted spies and available for our service.

22. It is through the information brought by the converted spy that we can acquire and employ local and inward spies.

23. It is owing to his information, again, that we can cause the doomed spy to carry false tidings to the enemy.

24. Lastly, it is by his information that the surviving spy can be used on appointed occasions.

25. The end and aim of spying in all its five varieties is knowledge of the enemy; and this knowledge can only be derived, in the first instance, from the converted spy. Hence it is essential that the converted spy be treated with the utmost liberality.

26. Of old, the rise of the Yin dynasty was because I Chih who had served under the Hsia. Likewise, the rise of the Chou dynasty was due to Lü Ya who had served under the Yin.

27. Hence it is only the enlightened ruler and the wise general who will use the highest intelligence of the army for purposes of spying and thereby they achieve great results. Spies are a most important element in war, because on them depends on an army's ability to move.

SECTION 2

IMPLICATIONS FOR HR LEADERS

I. APPLYING SUN TZU'S "LAYING PLANS" TO HR

I. Introduction

Strategic planning in human resources (HR) is crucial for organizational success. Like the art of war, where careful planning can determine the outcome, strategic HR management is vital for gaining and maintaining a competitive advantage. Sun Tzu's "The Art of War" provides timeless principles that can be applied to modern HR practices. This essay explores how the principles of "Laying Plans" from Sun Tzu's classic work can guide HR professionals in building effective strategies to navigate workforce dynamics.

II. The Five Constant Factors

The Moral Law (Organizational Culture)

Sun Tzu emphasizes the Moral Law as the foundation for unity and loyalty. In HR, this translates to ensuring that employees align with the company's values and mission. A strong organizational culture fosters a cohesive and motivated workforce, reducing turnover and enhancing overall performance.

Heaven (External Environment)

Heaven refers to external factors such as market conditions, economic cycles, and technological advancements. HR must adapt to these changes by staying informed about industry trends and preparing for uncertainties. This involves developing strategies that can respond to shifts in the external environment, ensuring the organization remains competitive.

Earth (Internal Environment)

Earth encompasses the internal environment, including organizational structure, resource availability, and operational conditions. HR needs to understand the company's internal dynamics to assess risks and opportunities effectively. By leveraging internal data, HR can identify areas for improvement and develop strategies to enhance organizational efficiency.

The Commander (Leadership)

The Commander signifies leadership qualities such as wisdom, sincerity, benevolence, courage, and discipline. Effective leaders are crucial in guiding and motivating employees. HR's role includes identifying and developing leaders who can embody these virtues and lead the organization toward its goals.

Method and Discipline (Processes and Systems)

Method and Discipline involve establishing clear procedures and workflows. This includes maintaining efficient communication, managing resources effectively, and monitoring performance. Structured processes ensure that HR operations run smoothly and support the organization's strategic objectives.

III. Applying the Five Constant Factors in HR Planning

Comparison and Evaluation

HR must continuously assess and evaluate its alignment with the five constant factors:

- Organizational Culture (Moral Law): Ensure recruitment and talent management strategies reflect the company's values.
- Leadership (The Commander): Evaluate the effectiveness of leaders and their impact on the workforce.
- External Environment (Heaven): Analyze market conditions and adapt HR strategies accordingly.
- Internal Environment (Earth): Assess internal resources and operational conditions to identify risks

and opportunities.
- Processes and Systems (Method and Discipline): Ensure that HR processes are efficient and support organizational goals.

Forecasting and Strategic Planning
Using Sun Tzu's seven considerations for predicting outcomes can enhance HR strategic planning:

- Alignment with Moral Law: Ensure employees share the organization's values.
- Leadership Abilities: Develop and support effective leaders.
- Environmental Advantages: Adapt to external conditions.
- Discipline Enforcement: Maintain rigorous standards.
- Organizational Strength: Build a strong workforce.
- Training and Development: Invest in employee growth.
- Consistency in Rewards and Punishments: Ensure fair and transparent practices.

IV. Flexibility and Adaptation

Adapting Plans Based on Circumstances
HR strategies must be flexible to respond to changing conditions. This involves regularly reviewing and adjusting plans to leverage favorable situations and address challenges. By remaining adaptable, HR can effectively manage uncertainties and maintain a strategic advantage.

Deception and Strategic Maneuvering
In a competitive landscape, HR can use strategic maneuvering to stay ahead. This includes gathering competitive intelligence and implementing initiatives that differentiate the organization. Strategic HR actions can create a competitive edge, making it harder for competitors to replicate success.

V. Preparation and Calculations

Importance of Thorough Planning
Thorough planning and forecasting are critical in HR strategy.

By calculating risks and potential outcomes, HR can make informed decisions that drive organizational success. Detailed plans provide a roadmap for achieving strategic goals and navigating challenges.

Learning from Success and Failure

Analyzing past HR initiatives helps identify what works and what doesn't. Continuous improvement and learning from both successes and failures are essential for refining strategies and achieving long-term success.

VI. Practical Applications in HR

Recruitment and Talent Management

Aligning Recruitment Strategies with Organizational Culture and Values (Moral Law): Recruiting individuals who align with the company's values ensures cultural fit and enhances employee engagement. This involves not just evaluating skills and experience, but also assessing candidates' alignment with the company's mission and values. Tools like cultural fit assessments and behavioral interviews can help in identifying the right candidates.

Adapting Recruitment Tactics to Changing Market Conditions and Workforce Trends (Heaven): Stay agile by adjusting recruitment strategies to reflect market dynamics. For instance, during economic downturns, focus on attracting top talent from competitors. During periods of rapid technological advancement, prioritize candidates with cutting-edge skills.

Utilizing Internal Data to Identify Talent Gaps and Opportunities (Earth): Leverage internal data to identify areas for improvement and target recruitment efforts. This includes using workforce analytics to understand turnover trends, employee satisfaction, and skills gaps. By doing so, HR can proactively address potential shortages and ensure a steady pipeline of talent.

Training and Developing Leadership within the HR Team (The Commander): Invest in leadership development to build a strong HR team. This can be achieved through mentorship programs, leadership workshops, and continuous learning opportunities. Strong HR leadership ensures that the team can effectively support the organization's strategic goals.

Implementing Efficient Recruitment Processes and Systems (Method and Discipline): Streamline recruitment processes to enhance efficiency and effectiveness. This involves using technology like applicant tracking systems (ATS) to manage the hiring process, reducing time-to-hire, and improving the candidate experience. Standardized procedures also help in maintaining consistency and fairness in hiring decisions.

Employee Engagement and Retention

Fostering a Positive and Cohesive Workplace Culture (Moral Law): Create a supportive environment that promotes employee satisfaction and loyalty. This includes recognizing and rewarding employee contributions, promoting work-life balance, and ensuring a safe and inclusive workplace.

Creating Engagement Strategies that Adapt to Different Employee Needs and External Factors (Heaven): Develop flexible engagement strategies to meet diverse employee needs. This could involve offering remote work options, flexible hours, and personalized development plans.

Assessing Internal Factors such as Team Dynamics and Work Environment (Earth): Regularly evaluate internal factors to enhance the work environment. Use employee surveys, focus groups, and feedback sessions to gather insights on team dynamics and organizational climate.

Developing Leadership Programs to Enhance Employee Motivation and Loyalty (The Commander): Implement leadership programs that motivate and retain employees. These programs should focus on developing leadership skills at all levels, from entry-level employees to senior executives.

Establishing Clear Communication Channels and Feedback Systems (Method and Discipline): Ensure open communication and feedback mechanisms to support employee engagement. This includes regular check-ins, performance reviews, and anonymous feedback channels to address employee concerns promptly.

Performance Management

Setting Performance Expectations Aligned with Organizational Goals (Moral Law): Define clear performance expectations that align with the company's objectives. Use goal-setting frameworks like OKRs (Objectives and Key Results) to ensure that individual and team goals contribute to the overall strategic vision.

Adapting Performance Management Practices to Evolving Business Conditions (Heaven): Adjust performance management practices to reflect changing business needs. This might involve updating performance criteria, introducing flexible performance metrics, and incorporating 360-degree feedback.

Monitoring Internal Performance Data to Identify Strengths and Areas for Improvement (Earth): Use performance data to guide improvements. Implement performance dashboards that provide real-time insights into individual and team performance, enabling timely interventions.

Ensuring Leaders are Equipped to Manage and Motivate their Teams Effectively (The Commander): Provide leaders with the tools and training they need to manage teams effectively. This includes leadership development programs, coaching, and access to performance management tools.

Implementing Structured Performance Review Processes and Reward Systems (Method and Discipline): Establish fair and consistent performance review processes and reward systems. Regular performance reviews, coupled with clear reward criteria, help in recognizing and motivating high performers.

Change Management

Communicating the Importance of Change Initiatives to Gain Employee Buy-in (Moral Law): Clearly communicate the reasons for change to secure employee support. Use transparent and consistent messaging to explain the benefits and necessity of change initiatives.

Preparing for External Changes and Uncertainties that May Impact the Organization (Heaven): Develop strategies to manage external changes. This includes scenario planning, risk assessments, and creating contingency plans to address potential disruptions.

Assessing Internal Readiness and Potential Obstacles to Change (Earth): Evaluate the organization's readiness for change and identify potential obstacles. Conduct readiness assessments, gather employee feedback, and identify change champions within the organization.

Leading Change Initiatives with Clear Vision and Strong Leadership (The Commander): Guide change with a clear vision and effective leadership. Leaders should articulate a compelling vision for change, engage employees at all levels, and demonstrate commitment to the change process.

Establishing Frameworks for Managing and Sustaining Change (Method and Discipline): Implement frameworks to manage and sustain change initiatives. Use change management models like Kotter's 8-Step Process or ADKAR (Awareness, Desire, Knowledge, Ability, Reinforcement) to ensure structured and sustainable change efforts.

Learning and Development
Aligning Learning and Development Programs with Organizational Values and Strategic Goals (Moral Law): Ensure training programs support the company's values and goals. This involves aligning learning objectives with organizational priorities and promoting a culture of continuous learning.

Adapting Training Programs to Current Industry Trends and Technological Advancements (Heaven): Update training programs to reflect industry trends. Incorporate e-learning, virtual training sessions, and AI-powered learning platforms to keep training content relevant and accessible.

Identifying Internal Skills Gaps and Development Opportunities (Earth): Use internal data to identify skill gaps and development opportunities. Conduct skills assessments, career development discussions, and leverage learning management systems (LMS) to track progress.

Ensuring Leaders are Involved in Mentoring and Developing their Teams (The Commander): Encourage leaders to mentor and develop their teams. Create formal mentoring programs, peer learning groups, and leadership coaching initiatives to support employee development.

Creating Structured Training Programs and Career Development Paths (Method and Discipline): Develop clear training programs and career paths to support employee growth. Offer a mix of formal training, on-the-job learning, and career progression frameworks to help employees advance.

VII. Future Trends and Considerations

Technological Advancements

AI and automation are transforming HR practices. Preparing for the future of work involves strategic planning to integrate these technologies effectively, ensuring that HR remains adaptive and competitive.

AI in Recruitment: AI-powered tools can streamline the recruitment process by automating resume screening, matching candidates to job descriptions, and even conducting initial interviews using chatbots.

Automation in Performance Management: Automated performance management systems can track employee progress, provide real-time feedback, and identify areas for development without manual intervention.

Learning and Development: AI can personalize learning experiences by recommending training modules based on an employee's performance data and career aspirations.

Globalization and Diversity

Managing a diverse and global workforce requires adapting HR strategies to different cultural and regulatory environments. Embracing diversity and inclusion enhances organizational innovation and performance.

Cultural Competence: HR professionals must develop cultural

competence to manage a diverse workforce effectively. This includes understanding cultural norms, communication styles, and workplace expectations.

Regulatory Compliance: Global operations require compliance with various labor laws and regulations. HR must stay informed about these requirements to avoid legal pitfalls.

Inclusive Policies: Developing inclusive policies and practices ensures that all employees feel valued and supported, regardless of their background.

Sustainability and Corporate Social Responsibility

Integrating sustainability into HR strategies promotes ethical practices and social responsibility. HR can lead initiatives that support environmental sustainability and corporate social responsibility, aligning with broader organizational goals.

Green HR Practices: Implementing eco-friendly practices such as remote work policies, digital documentation, and sustainable office environments can reduce the company's carbon footprint.

Ethical Recruitment: HR can promote ethical recruitment practices by ensuring fair treatment of all candidates and avoiding discrimination.

CSR Initiatives: HR can support CSR initiatives by encouraging employee participation in community service, sustainability projects, and ethical business practices.

VIII. Conclusion

Strategic HR planning is essential for organizational success. Applying Sun Tzu's principles, such as aligning with organizational culture, adapting to external conditions, leveraging internal data, and developing strong leadership, can enhance HR practices and outcomes.

HR professionals should adopt a strategic mindset, continuously learning and adapting to ensure that their organizations remain competitive and resilient. By integrating Sun Tzu's principles, HR can navigate the complexities of the modern workforce and drive organizational success.

II APPLYING SUN TZU'S "WAGING WAR" TO HR

I. Introduction

Strategic planning and efficiency in human resources (HR) management are critical to the success and sustainability of any organization. Just as in warfare, where the effective use of resources and swift execution of plans can determine the outcome, strategic HR management requires careful consideration of resource allocation, process optimization, and timely decision-making. Sun Tzu's "The Art of War" offers timeless principles that can be applied to modern HR practices, particularly in the context of resource management and operational efficiency. This essay explores how the concepts from Sun Tzu's chapter "Waging War" can guide HR professionals in optimizing their strategies and operations.

II. Resource Management

Understanding the Costs (Provision and Expenditure)

Sun Tzu begins by outlining the substantial costs associated with raising and maintaining an army. Similarly, HR operations involve significant investments in recruitment, training, employee development, and other activities. It is essential for HR professionals to fully understand these costs to manage them effectively.

HR must evaluate the full cost of their initiatives, including direct expenses like salaries and benefits, and indirect costs such as training, employee turnover, and productivity losses. This comprehensive assessment helps in budgeting and ensures that resources are allocated efficiently. Just as the costs of war can strain a state's resources, extensive HR initiatives can impact an organization's financial health. HR must balance investments in people with the organization's budget constraints to avoid financial strain.

Avoiding Protracted Campaigns

Sun Tzu warns against prolonged warfare, which can drain resources and dampen morale. In HR, prolonged processes and unresolved issues can lead to inefficiencies and lower employee engagement.

HR should streamline recruitment, onboarding, and training processes to reduce time and costs. Efficient processes help maintain momentum and ensure that employees are productive from the start. Addressing employee concerns and resolving conflicts promptly prevents prolonged dissatisfaction and disengagement. Quick action maintains high morale and productivity.

III. Impact of Prolonged Efforts

Dulling of Tools and Dampening of Ardor

Prolonged efforts can lead to the dulling of tools and dampening of ardor, as Sun Tzu notes. In HR, this translates to burnout and disengagement among both HR staff and employees.

Implementing measures to prevent burnout, such as reasonable workloads, sufficient breaks, and support systems, helps maintain energy and motivation among HR staff and employees. Regular recognition and rewards, along with opportunities for career development, keep employees motivated and engaged, reducing the risk of dampened ardor.

Exhaustion of Strength and Resources

Prolonged efforts can also exhaust an organization's strength and resources, leading to inefficiency and vulnerability. HR must continuously monitor the allocation of resources to prevent depletion. This involves tracking expenditures, evaluating the effectiveness of initiatives, and reallocating resources as needed.

Implementing sustainable HR practices, such as continuous improvement and lean management techniques, ensures long-term viability and efficiency.

IV. Strategic Efficiency

Avoiding Multiple Levies

Sun Tzu emphasizes the importance of avoiding multiple levies, or repeated calls for resources. In HR, this principle translates to maximizing the effectiveness of initial investments and avoiding unnecessary additional expenditures.

HR should focus on making the most of initial investments in recruitment, training, and development. This can be achieved by thoroughly vetting candidates, providing comprehensive onboarding, and offering continuous learning opportunities. Before seeking additional resources, HR should ensure that existing resources are used efficiently. This includes optimizing workflows, eliminating redundancies, and leveraging technology to enhance productivity.

Foraging on the Enemy

Sun Tzu advises foraging on the enemy to sustain the army. In HR, this can be interpreted as leveraging external resources and best practices to supplement internal efforts.

HR can benefit from external resources such as industry benchmarks, best practices, and competitive intelligence. This helps in staying updated with industry trends and adopting proven strategies. Comparing HR practices with those of competitors provides valuable insights into areas for improvement and innovation. This strategic maneuvering ensures that the organization remains competitive.

V. Economic Considerations

Avoiding Impoverishment

Sun Tzu highlights the risk of impoverishment due to sustained warfare. Similarly, extensive HR initiatives can strain an organization's finances if not managed carefully.

HR must ensure that the costs of initiatives are justified by the benefits. This involves conducting cost-benefit analyses and prioritizing initiatives that offer the highest return on investment. By keeping HR expenditures in check, organizations can maintain overall financial health. This balance is crucial for sustaining operations and supporting growth.

Managing the Economic Impact of HR Operations

The economic impact of HR operations extends beyond direct costs. It also includes the effects on organizational productivity, employee morale, and retention.

HR should develop strategies to mitigate the economic impact of their operations. This includes optimizing recruitment and training processes, reducing turnover, and enhancing employee productivity. Implementing cost-effective HR strategies, such as leveraging technology for training and development, helps in managing costs without compromising quality.

VI. Incentivizing Success

Rewarding Achievements

Sun Tzu stresses the importance of rewarding those who achieve success in battle. In HR, recognizing and rewarding achievements is key to maintaining motivation and encouraging high performance.

Implementing recognition programs that reward employees for their contributions boosts morale and motivation. These programs should be fair, transparent, and aligned with organizational goals. Offering performance-based incentives, such as bonuses and promotions, encourages employees to strive for excellence. These incentives should be tied to clear, measurable performance criteria.

Integrating New Resources

Sun Tzu advises using captured resources to augment one's own strength. In HR, this principle can be applied to effectively integrating new hires and resources into the organization.

Providing comprehensive onboarding programs ensures that new hires are quickly integrated into the organization and productive from the start. This includes orientation, training, and mentorship. When acquiring talent through mergers or acquisitions, HR should focus on effectively integrating new employees into the existing workforce. This involves understanding their strengths and aligning them with organizational needs.

VII. Maintaining Focus on Victory

Achieving Objectives Efficiently

Sun Tzu emphasizes the importance of achieving objectives efficiently rather than engaging in prolonged campaigns. In HR, this means setting clear, achievable goals and working towards them systematically.

HR should set clear, measurable goals that align with organizational objectives. This ensures that all efforts are directed towards achieving strategic priorities. Implementing structured plans and processes helps in achieving goals efficiently. This involves breaking down goals into manageable tasks, assigning responsibilities, and monitoring progress.

Leadership's Role in HR Success

Sun Tzu underscores the critical role of leadership in determining the outcome of warfare. Similarly, effective HR leadership is crucial for the success of HR initiatives and overall organizational performance.

HR leaders must be strategic thinkers who can align HR initiatives with organizational goals. This involves understanding the broader business context and making informed decisions. Engaging employees through effective communication, support, and development opportunities is a key responsibility of HR leaders. This engagement drives motivation and productivity, contributing to organizational success.

VIII. Practical Applications in HR

1. Workforce Planning

Sun Tzu's discussion on the immense logistical demands and costs of maintaining an army can be mirrored in the strategic HR practice of workforce planning. Effective workforce planning requires a thorough understanding of the current and future needs of the organization, as well as the costs associated with maintaining and developing a skilled workforce. This involves not only the direct costs of salaries and benefits but also indirect costs such as training, development programs, and potential turnover.

HR must ensure that the organization has the right number of employees with the right skills at the right time. This can be achieved through comprehensive workforce analysis, identifying critical roles and skills required to meet future business objectives, and developing a strategic plan to bridge any gaps. By doing so, HR can avoid the pitfalls of overstaffing or understaffing, which can strain financial resources and hinder organizational performance. Implementing strategic workforce planning helps maintain a balance between supply and demand, ensuring that the organization remains agile and capable of responding to changing market conditions. By applying Sun Tzu's principles of efficient resource management, HR can optimize workforce planning processes to support long-term organizational success.

2. Learning and Development

Sun Tzu's emphasis on avoiding prolonged campaigns and the associated risks of resource depletion can be applied to HR's approach to learning and development. Prolonged training programs that are not aligned with the organization's immediate needs can lead to wasted resources and disengaged employees. HR should adopt a more strategic approach to learning and development, focusing on creating concise, impactful training programs that address current skill gaps and future needs.

To ensure training programs are effective and efficient, HR can leverage technology and e-learning platforms to provide on-demand, modular training that employees can access as needed. This approach not only reduces the time and cost associated with traditional classroom training but also allows employees to learn at their own pace and apply new skills directly to their roles. Furthermore, integrating continuous learning opportunities, such as microlearning modules and just-in-time training, ensures that employees remain engaged and their skills stay relevant. By aligning learning and development initiatives with organizational goals and avoiding prolonged, ineffective training programs, HR can maintain a highly skilled and agile workforce, much like a skilled general who keeps his army well-prepared and resourceful.

3. Change Management

Sun Tzu's insights on avoiding prolonged campaigns and the exhaustion of resources are particularly relevant to HR's role in managing organizational change. Prolonged and poorly managed change initiatives can lead to employee resistance, burnout, and a depletion of organizational resources. HR must approach change management with a strategic mindset, ensuring that changes are implemented efficiently and with minimal disruption. This involves thorough planning, clear communication, and engaging employees throughout the process to gain their buy-in and support. HR should also provide the necessary training and resources to help employees adapt to new systems, processes, or structures, reducing the strain and anxiety associated with change. Monitoring the impact of change initiatives and being agile enough to adjust as needed can prevent prolonged periods of uncertainty and instability. By following these principles, HR can manage change effectively, maintaining organizational strength and employee morale, in line with Sun Tzu's emphasis on the importance of strategic efficiency and resource management in warfare.

4. Succession Planning

Sun Tzu's principle of avoiding multiple levies or repeated calls for resources can be applied to HR's approach to succession planning. In HR, this principle translates to ensuring that the organization is prepared for leadership transitions without repeatedly scrambling to fill critical roles. Succession planning involves identifying and developing internal candidates who can step into key positions when needed, thereby reducing the disruption and costs associated with external recruitment.

HR should implement a robust succession planning process that includes identifying high-potential employees, providing them with targeted development opportunities, and creating clear career pathways. This proactive approach ensures that the organization has a pipeline of qualified leaders ready to take on new challenges, thereby minimizing the risk of leadership gaps. Additionally, succession planning should be integrated with overall workforce planning to ensure alignment with the organization's strategic goals. By maintaining a strong focus on succession planning, HR can avoid the inefficiencies and costs associated with repeated external recruitment, much like a general who avoids the need for multiple levies by keeping his army well-prepared and adequately resourced.

5. Recruitment and Talent Management

Aligning recruitment strategies with organizational culture and values (Moral Law) is essential. Recruiting individuals who align with the company's values ensures cultural fit and enhances employee engagement. This involves not just evaluating skills and experience, but also assessing candidates' alignment with the company's mission and values. Tools like cultural fit assessments and behavioral interviews can help in identifying the right candidates.

HR must adapt recruitment tactics to changing market conditions and workforce trends (Heaven). Staying agile by adjusting recruitment strategies to reflect market dynamics is crucial. For instance, during economic downturns, focus on attracting top talent from competitors. During periods of rapid technological advancement, prioritize candidates with cutting-edge skills.

Utilizing internal data to identify talent gaps and opportunities (Earth) is another critical strategy. Leveraging internal data to identify areas for improvement and target recruitment efforts helps HR proactively address potential shortages and ensure a steady pipeline of talent.

Training and developing leadership within the HR team (The Commander) builds a strong HR team. This can be achieved through mentorship programs, leadership workshops, and continuous learning opportunities. Strong HR leadership ensures that the team can effectively support the organization's strategic goals.

Implementing efficient recruitment processes and systems (Method and Discipline) enhances efficiency and effectiveness. This involves using technology like applicant tracking systems (ATS) to manage the hiring process, reducing time-to-hire, and improving the candidate experience. Standardized procedures also help in maintaining consistency and fairness in hiring decisions.

IX. Conclusion

Strategic HR planning is essential for organizational success. Applying Sun Tzu's principles, such as aligning with organizational culture, adapting to external conditions, leveraging internal data, and developing strong leadership, can enhance HR practices and outcomes. HR professionals should adopt a strategic mindset, continuously learning and adapting to ensure that their organizations remain competitive and resilient. By integrating Sun Tzu's principles, HR can navigate the complexities of the modern workforce and drive organizational success.

III. APPLYING SUN TZU'S "ATTACK BY STRATAGEM" TO HR

I. Introduction

Strategic planning and efficiency in human resources (HR) management are critical to the success and sustainability of any organization. Just as in warfare, where the effective use of resources and swift execution of plans can determine the outcome, strategic HR management requires careful consideration of resource allocation, process optimization, and timely decision-making. Sun Tzu's "The Art of War" offers timeless principles that can be applied to modern HR practices, particularly in the context of resource management and operational efficiency. This essay explores how the concepts from Sun Tzu's chapter "Attack by Stratagem" can guide HR professionals in optimizing their strategies and operations.

II. Strategic HR Management

Preserving Organizational Strength

Sun Tzu emphasizes the importance of capturing the enemy's resources intact rather than destroying them. In HR, this translates to preserving the strength and morale of the workforce rather than allowing conflicts and issues to erode it.

HR should focus on resolving conflicts and addressing issues without causing disruption or resentment among employees. This involves fostering open communication, mediation, and conflict resolution strategies that maintain harmony within the organization. By preserving the workforce's integrity, HR can ensure that employees remain engaged and productive.

Breaking Resistance Without Conflict

Sun Tzu states that supreme excellence consists in breaking the enemy's resistance without fighting. In HR, this principle can be applied to overcoming resistance to change and new initiatives without confrontation.

HR should adopt strategies that address employee concerns and build buy-in for new initiatives. This can be achieved through transparent communication, involving employees in the decision-making process, and highlighting the benefits of the changes. By proactively addressing resistance, HR can implement changes smoothly and effectively.

III. Tactical Avoidance and Strategic Engagement

Avoiding Protracted and Costly Conflicts

Sun Tzu warns against besieging walled cities, as it leads to prolonged and costly conflicts. In HR, this principle translates to avoiding long, drawn-out disputes and focusing on swift resolution.

HR should prioritize addressing issues and conflicts promptly to prevent them from escalating. This involves having clear policies and procedures for conflict resolution, as well as training managers to handle disputes effectively. By resolving issues quickly, HR can maintain a positive work environment and prevent prolonged disruptions.

Strategic Deployment of Resources

Sun Tzu advises deploying resources strategically based on the situation. In HR, this means tailoring strategies to the specific needs and circumstances of the organization and workforce.

HR must assess the strengths and weaknesses of their team and deploy resources where they are most needed. This involves understanding the unique needs of different departments and employee groups and providing targeted support and resources. By being strategic in resource allocation, HR can maximize impact and efficiency.

IV. Adapting to Circumstances

Understanding Organizational Dynamics

Sun Tzu emphasizes the importance of knowing both the enemy and oneself. In HR, this translates to understanding the internal dynamics of the organization as well as external factors affecting it.

HR should conduct regular assessments of employee satisfaction, engagement, and performance. This involves using tools like surveys, focus groups, and performance metrics to gather insights. By understanding the internal state of the organization, HR can make informed decisions and tailor strategies to address specific needs.

Flexibility and Adaptation

Sun Tzu highlights the need for flexibility and adaptation in response to changing circumstances. In HR, this principle is crucial for managing a dynamic workforce and evolving business environment.

HR must remain flexible and adaptable, adjusting strategies as needed to respond to changes in the market, technology, and workforce demographics. This involves continuous learning and development, as well as staying abreast of industry trends and best practices. By being adaptable, HR can effectively navigate challenges and seize opportunities.

V. Leadership and Decision-Making

The Role of Leadership in HR Success

Sun Tzu underscores the critical role of leadership in determining the outcome of warfare. Similarly, effective HR leadership is crucial for the success of HR initiatives and overall organizational performance.

HR leaders must be strategic thinkers who can align HR initiatives with organizational goals. This involves understanding the broader business context and making informed decisions. Engaging employees through effective communication, support, and development opportunities is a key responsibility of HR leaders. This engagement drives motivation and productivity, contributing to organizational success.

Avoiding Common Leadership Pitfalls

Sun Tzu outlines several ways in which poor leadership can lead to disaster. In HR, these pitfalls can manifest as mismanagement and inefficiency.

HR leaders must avoid commanding actions that are not feasible, administering the organization without understanding its dynamics, and employing personnel without considering their suitability for specific roles. By being aware of these pitfalls, HR leaders can foster a supportive and effective work environment.

VI. Practical Applications in HR

1. Strategic Decision-Making with AI

Sun Tzu's principle of achieving victory without engaging in direct conflict translates to the use of AI in strategic decision-making within HR. The goal is to leverage AI to anticipate and address potential issues before they escalate, thereby maintaining harmony and efficiency in the workplace. By integrating AI into HR analytics, organizations can predict trends, identify potential areas of concern, and develop proactive strategies.

AI-driven analytics can provide deep insights into employee engagement, productivity, and retention. For example, AI can analyze patterns in employee data to predict turnover risks, allowing HR to intervene with targeted retention strategies. This approach aligns with Sun Tzu's concept of breaking the enemy's resistance without fighting—HR can address underlying issues and improve employee satisfaction without the need for drastic measures. Moreover, AI can assist in workforce planning by forecasting future skill requirements and identifying existing skill gaps. By preparing the workforce for future challenges, HR can ensure that the organization remains competitive and resilient, effectively capturing "the enemy's cities without laying siege to them."

2. Enhancing Employee Experience through AI

Sun Tzu's emphasis on avoiding prolonged and costly engagements can be applied to improving the employee experience through AI. AI technologies such as chatbots, virtual assistants, and personalized learning platforms can streamline HR processes, enhance employee support, and reduce administrative burdens. These tools provide quick and accurate responses to employee queries, facilitate seamless onboarding experiences, and offer tailored learning opportunities.

Implementing AI-driven solutions in HR operations allows for a more efficient and satisfying employee experience. For instance, AI-powered chatbots can handle routine inquiries about benefits, payroll, and policies, freeing up HR professionals to focus on more strategic tasks. Virtual assistants can guide new hires through the onboarding process, ensuring they have the necessary resources and information to become productive members of the team quickly. Personalized learning platforms can analyze individual employee data to recommend specific training modules, helping employees develop the skills they need for career growth. By leveraging AI to enhance the employee experience, HR can maintain high levels of engagement and productivity, much like a skillful leader who subdues the enemy's troops without any fighting.

3. Risk Management and Compliance

Sun Tzu's advice on knowing when to fight and when to avoid conflict applies to HR's approach to risk management and compliance. AI can be instrumental in identifying potential compliance issues and mitigating risks before they become significant problems. By continuously monitoring HR processes and employee behaviors, AI systems can detect anomalies and flag potential violations of company policies or legal regulations.

For example, AI can analyze communication patterns to identify instances of harassment or discrimination, allowing HR to intervene early and address the issue before it escalates. Additionally, AI can ensure that HR practices comply with evolving labor laws and regulations by automatically updating policies and procedures as needed. This proactive approach to risk management ensures that the organization remains compliant and minimizes legal and reputational risks. By using AI to anticipate and mitigate risks, HR can maintain a stable and compliant workforce, aligning with Sun Tzu's principle of capturing the enemy's forces without a lengthy battle.

4. Leadership Development and Succession Planning

Sun Tzu's concept of knowing both oneself and the enemy is crucial for leadership development and succession planning in the era of AI. AI can provide valuable insights into the strengths and weaknesses of current leaders and identify potential future leaders within the organization. Through AI-driven assessments and analytics, HR can evaluate leadership competencies, performance, and potential, ensuring that the organization is prepared for future leadership transitions.

AI can also facilitate personalized development plans for leaders, offering targeted training and development opportunities based on individual needs and career goals. By understanding the capabilities of current leaders and preparing future leaders effectively, HR can ensure that the organization's leadership pipeline remains strong and capable of driving strategic initiatives. This approach mirrors Sun Tzu's strategy of ensuring that one's own forces are prepared and capable, thus avoiding the need for reactive and potentially disruptive measures. By leveraging AI for leadership development and succession planning, HR can maintain a resilient and forward-looking leadership team, ready to meet the challenges of a dynamic business environment.

5.Recruitment and Talent Management

Aligning recruitment strategies with organizational culture and values is crucial for ensuring a good cultural fit and enhancing employee engagement. This involves evaluating not only candidates' skills and experience but also their alignment with the company's mission and values. Tools like cultural fit assessments and behavioral interviews can be instrumental in identifying the right candidates. Additionally, adapting recruitment tactics to changing market conditions and workforce trends is essential for staying agile. For instance, during economic downturns, the focus should be on attracting top talent from competitors, whereas, during periods of rapid technological advancement, priority should be given to candidates with cutting-edge skills. Leveraging internal data to identify talent gaps and opportunities is another key strategy. By using workforce analytics to understand turnover trends, employee satisfaction, and skills gaps, HR can proactively address potential shortages and ensure a steady pipeline of talent. Training and developing leadership within the HR team is also vital. Investing in leadership development through mentorship programs, leadership workshops, and continuous learning opportunities builds a strong HR team capable of effectively supporting the organization's strategic goals. Finally, implementing efficient recruitment processes and systems is necessary to enhance efficiency and effectiveness. Using technology like applicant tracking systems (ATS) to manage the hiring process can reduce time-to-hire and improve the candidate experience, while standardized procedures help maintain consistency and fairness in hiring decisions.

VII. Conclusion

Strategic HR planning is essential for organizational success. Applying Sun Tzu's principles, such as aligning with organizational culture, adapting to external conditions, leveraging internal data, and developing strong leadership, can enhance HR practices and outcomes. HR professionals should adopt a strategic mindset, continuously learning and adapting to ensure that their organizations remain competitive and resilient. By integrating Sun Tzu's principles, HR can navigate the complexities of the modern workforce and drive organizational success.

IV. APPLYING SUN TZU'S "TACTICAL DISPOSITIONS" TO HR

I. Introduction

Strategic planning and operational efficiency in human resources (HR) are paramount for the success and resilience of any organization. Drawing parallels from warfare, where strategic dispositions and tactics dictate outcomes, HR management requires meticulous planning, resource allocation, and the anticipation of challenges. Sun Tzu's "The Art of War" offers timeless principles that can be applied to modern HR practices, particularly in the context of defensive and offensive strategies. This essay explores how the concepts from Sun Tzu's chapter "Tactical Dispositions" can guide HR professionals in building robust strategies that ensure organizational success.

II. Ensuring Organizational Stability

Securing Against Defeat

Sun Tzu emphasizes the importance of first putting oneself beyond the possibility of defeat. In HR, this principle translates to creating a stable and resilient organizational foundation that can withstand internal and external challenges.

1. Strong Organizational Culture: Cultivating a strong organizational culture that aligns with the company's values and mission is crucial. This involves clear communication of the company's vision, regular reinforcement of core values,

and fostering an inclusive and supportive work environment. A strong culture acts as a defensive mechanism, promoting employee loyalty and reducing turnover.

2. Comprehensive Risk Management: HR must implement comprehensive risk management strategies to anticipate and mitigate potential threats. This includes conducting regular risk assessments, developing contingency plans, and ensuring compliance with legal and regulatory requirements. By proactively addressing risks, HR can safeguard the organization against disruptions.

3. Employee Well-being Programs: Prioritizing employee well-being is essential for maintaining a stable workforce. HR should implement programs that support physical, mental, and emotional health, such as wellness initiatives, employee assistance programs, and flexible work arrangements. A healthy and satisfied workforce is more resilient and less prone to stress-related issues.

Building Defensive Tactics

To secure the organization against defeat, HR must adopt defensive tactics that protect its interests and resources.

1. Robust Policies and Procedures: Establishing robust HR policies and procedures ensures consistency and fairness in managing employee relations. Clear guidelines on performance management, conflict resolution, and disciplinary actions help prevent misunderstandings and disputes, thereby maintaining organizational stability.

2. Talent Retention Strategies: Retaining top talent is a critical defensive tactic. HR should implement strategies to keep high-performing employees engaged and motivated, such as career development opportunities, competitive compensation packages, and recognition programs. Retaining key talent reduces the risk of skill gaps and maintains continuity in operations.

3. Effective Communication Channels: Maintaining open and transparent communication channels is vital for addressing employee concerns promptly. HR should facilitate regular feedback mechanisms, such as surveys and town hall meetings, to gauge employee sentiment and address issues before they escalate. Effective communication fosters trust and enhances organizational cohesion.

III. Capitalizing on Opportunities

Taking the Offensive

While securing against defeat is essential, HR must also be prepared to take offensive actions to seize opportunities for growth and improvement.

1. Proactive Talent Acquisition: HR should adopt proactive recruitment strategies to attract top talent. This includes building a strong employer brand, leveraging social media and professional networks, and participating in industry events. By actively seeking out talented individuals, HR can strengthen the organization's capabilities and gain a competitive edge.

2. Innovative Learning and Development Programs: Implementing innovative learning and development programs is an offensive strategy that enhances employee skills and fosters continuous improvement. HR should offer a variety of training opportunities, including online courses, workshops, and mentoring programs. Investing in employee development ensures that the workforce remains agile and capable of adapting to changing industry demands.

3. Performance Optimization: HR should focus on optimizing performance by setting clear goals and expectations, providing regular feedback, and conducting performance reviews. Utilizing performance management tools and software can streamline the process and provide actionable insights. Optimizing performance ensures that employees are productive

and aligned with organizational objectives.

IV. Balancing Defensive and Offensive Strategies

Strategic Flexibility

Sun Tzu highlights the importance of balancing defensive and offensive tactics. In HR, this balance is crucial for maintaining stability while pursuing opportunities.

1. Adaptive Leadership: HR leaders must be adaptive and flexible, capable of shifting between defensive and offensive strategies as needed. This involves staying informed about industry trends, anticipating market changes, and being prepared to pivot strategies in response to new challenges or opportunities.

2. Scenario Planning: Conducting scenario planning exercises helps HR prepare for various contingencies. By considering different scenarios and developing corresponding strategies, HR can ensure that the organization is ready to respond effectively to both threats and opportunities.

3. Resource Allocation: Effective resource allocation is key to balancing defensive and offensive strategies. HR must ensure that resources are allocated efficiently to support both stability and growth initiatives. This includes budgeting for employee development programs, technology investments, and risk management efforts.

Measurement and Evaluation

Sun Tzu's principle of measurement, estimation, calculation, balancing chances, and achieving victory applies directly to HR's need for data-driven decision-making.

1. HR Metrics and Analytics: Utilizing HR metrics and analytics enables HR to measure and evaluate the effectiveness of their strategies. Key performance indicators (KPIs) such as employee engagement, turnover rates, and training ROI provide valuable insights into organizational health and performance.

2. Continuous Improvement: HR should foster a culture of continuous improvement by regularly reviewing and refining policies, processes, and programs. This involves gathering feedback from employees, analyzing performance data, and making data-driven adjustments. Continuous improvement ensures that HR strategies remain effective and aligned with organizational goals.

3. Benchmarking: Comparing HR practices with industry benchmarks helps HR identify areas for improvement and adopt best practices. Benchmarking against similar organizations provides a reference point for evaluating performance and identifying opportunities for enhancement.

V. Cultivating Excellence

Excellence in Execution

Sun Tzu states that true excellence lies in winning with ease and making no mistakes. In HR, this translates to executing strategies flawlessly and avoiding common pitfalls.

1. Attention to Detail: HR must pay close attention to detail in all aspects of their work, from policy implementation to employee relations. Thorough planning, meticulous execution, and regular monitoring help ensure that HR initiatives are carried out effectively and without errors.

2. Best Practices: Adopting best practices in HR management is essential for achieving excellence. This includes staying updated with industry trends, attending professional development events, and participating in HR networks and forums. By continuously learning and adopting proven strategies, HR can enhance their effectiveness and efficiency.

3. Empowering Employees: Empowering employees to take ownership of their work and contribute to organizational success is a hallmark of excellence. HR should create an environment where employees feel valued, supported, and

empowered to innovate and excel. This involves providing autonomy, encouraging collaboration, and recognizing achievements.

Cultivating Moral Law and Discipline

Sun Tzu emphasizes the importance of adhering to moral law and discipline. In HR, this principle is reflected in ethical practices and consistent application of policies.

1. Ethical Leadership: HR leaders must demonstrate ethical leadership by acting with integrity, fairness, and transparency. Ethical leadership sets the tone for the organization and fosters a culture of trust and respect.

2. Consistency in Policy Enforcement: Consistent enforcement of HR policies is crucial for maintaining discipline and fairness. HR must ensure that policies are applied uniformly across the organization, without favoritism or bias. Consistency builds trust and credibility, reinforcing the organization's values.

3. Accountability: Holding employees and leaders accountable for their actions is essential for maintaining discipline. HR should establish clear expectations and consequences for behavior that aligns with or deviates from organizational values. Accountability reinforces the importance of ethical conduct and supports a positive work environment.

VI. Practical Applications in HR

1. Proactive Risk Management

Sun Tzu's principle of securing oneself against defeat before seeking victory can be directly applied to HR's approach to risk management. Effective HR risk management involves identifying potential risks and mitigating them proactively. This includes recognizing compliance issues, employee dissatisfaction, and operational inefficiencies before they escalate into significant problems.

HR departments should establish comprehensive risk

management protocols that monitor and address these potential issues. For instance, by regularly reviewing and updating company policies to ensure compliance with labor laws, HR can prevent legal disputes and protect the organization's reputation. Additionally, HR should implement systems to gauge employee morale and satisfaction through surveys and feedback mechanisms. Identifying and addressing areas of concern early helps maintain a positive work environment and prevents larger issues from arising. By managing risks proactively, HR can secure the organization against potential defeats, much like a skilled general who fortifies his position before engaging the enemy.

2. Strategic Decision-Making

Sun Tzu's emphasis on measurement, estimation, calculation, and balancing of chances to achieve victory aligns with strategic decision-making in HR. Effective HR management relies on thorough analysis and planning to make informed decisions that drive organizational success.

HR should utilize data analytics to gain insights into workforce trends, employee performance, and organizational health. For example, analyzing data on employee turnover can reveal patterns and underlying causes, enabling HR to develop targeted retention strategies. Additionally, understanding the impact of various HR initiatives, such as training programs or policy changes, allows for better planning and resource allocation. By calculating potential outcomes and balancing risks and benefits, HR can implement strategies that are more likely to succeed. This methodical approach to decision-making ensures that HR initiatives are well-informed and strategically aligned with organizational goals, mirroring Sun Tzu's strategy of ensuring victory through careful planning and positioning.

3. Building a Resilient Organizational Culture

Sun Tzu's concept of cultivating the moral law and adhering to method and discipline can be applied to building a resilient organizational culture. A strong culture is fundamental to an organization's success, promoting employee engagement, satisfaction, and productivity.

HR plays a crucial role in fostering a positive and inclusive workplace culture by promoting transparency, accountability, and continuous improvement. This involves implementing and enforcing consistent policies and practices that reflect the organization's values. HR should also actively gather and analyze employee feedback to identify areas for cultural improvement. For example, regular surveys and focus groups can provide insights into employee perceptions and experiences. Addressing any issues promptly helps to reinforce a cohesive and supportive culture. By maintaining discipline in policy implementation and continuously promoting organizational values, HR can build and sustain a resilient culture that supports the organization's long-term success, much like a disciplined general who ensures his forces are well-prepared and unified.

4. Strategic Workforce Optimization

Sun Tzu's principle of making no mistakes and ensuring victory by conquering an already defeated enemy can be applied to strategic workforce optimization in HR. Effective workforce management involves identifying inefficiencies and optimizing resources to ensure maximum productivity and effectiveness.

HR should conduct regular workforce analysis to identify skill gaps and optimize resource allocation. This includes developing strategic hiring and training plans that align with the organization's goals. For instance, by analyzing workforce data, HR can forecast future skill requirements and address potential shortages proactively. Additionally, HR should streamline workforce management processes, such as scheduling and performance reviews, to enhance overall productivity. Implementing efficient workflows and eliminating redundancies ensures that the organization operates smoothly and effectively. By optimizing workforce management, HR can position the organization for success, much like a skillful fighter who secures victory by making no mistakes.

5. Real-Time Monitoring and Adaptation

Sun Tzu's teaching on the importance of being able to protect oneself and take decisive action when the moment is right can be applied to real-time monitoring and adaptation in HR. Effective HR management requires agility to respond quickly to changing conditions and emerging challenges.

HR should establish mechanisms for continuous monitoring of various aspects of the workforce and organizational environment. This includes tracking employee sentiment, productivity, and the effectiveness of HR initiatives. For example, real-time feedback tools and regular check-ins can provide immediate insights into employee morale and engagement. By monitoring these indicators, HR can identify issues as they arise and implement timely interventions to address them. This proactive approach ensures that HR can maintain organizational stability and readiness, responding to challenges and opportunities as they occur, much like a general who waits for the perfect moment to strike from a position of strength.

By focusing on these strategic applications, HR can enhance its effectiveness, drive organizational success, and ensure that the organization remains resilient and competitive.

VII. Conclusion

Strategic HR planning is essential for organizational success. Applying Sun Tzu's principles, such as securing against defeat, capitalizing on opportunities, balancing defensive and offensive strategies, and cultivating excellence, can enhance HR practices and outcomes. HR professionals should adopt a strategic mindset, continuously learning and adapting to ensure that their organizations remain competitive and resilient.

By integrating Sun Tzu's principles, HR can navigate the complexities of the modern workforce and drive organizational success.

V. APPLYING SUN TZU'S "ENERGY" TO HR

I. Introduction

Effective human resources (HR) management is essential for the success and sustainability of any organization. Sun Tzu's "The Art of War" offers timeless principles that can be applied to modern HR practices, particularly in the context of energy management. This essay explores how the concepts from Sun Tzu's chapter "Energy" can guide HR professionals in optimizing their strategies and operations to harness and direct the collective energy of the workforce.

II. Harnessing Collective Energy

Division and Coordination

Sun Tzu begins by asserting that the control of a large force is based on the same principles as the control of a few men; it is merely a question of dividing up their numbers. In HR, this principle emphasizes the importance of organizational structure and coordination. Effective division of labor and clear communication channels are essential for managing a large workforce. HR must ensure that roles and responsibilities are clearly defined and that there are systems in place to facilitate coordination among different teams and departments.

HR can implement this by creating detailed job descriptions, setting up efficient communication systems, and ensuring that there are regular meetings and updates. By doing so, HR can ensure that every employee understands their role within the larger organizational framework and can collaborate effectively with others. This division and coordination help maintain organizational efficiency and prevent confusion and duplication of efforts.

Direct and Indirect Methods

Sun Tzu highlights the importance of using both direct and indirect methods to achieve success. In HR, this translates to a combination of straightforward management practices and more subtle, strategic interventions. Direct methods include clear policies, procedures, and performance metrics. These provide a framework within which employees can operate and understand what is expected of them.

Indirect methods, on the other hand, involve more nuanced approaches such as fostering a positive organizational culture, using motivational techniques, and implementing change management strategies. These methods are aimed at influencing employee behavior and attitudes in a less direct but equally effective manner. By combining direct and indirect methods, HR can create a dynamic and responsive work environment that adapts to challenges and opportunities.

III. Leveraging Strengths and Weaknesses

Identifying Weak Points and Strong Points

Sun Tzu emphasizes the importance of understanding the science of weak points and strong points. For HR, this means identifying the strengths and weaknesses within the workforce and the organization. This requires a thorough assessment of employee skills, competencies, and performance levels, as well as an understanding of organizational capabilities and limitations.

HR can use tools such as performance appraisals, skills assessments, and employee feedback surveys to gather this information. By identifying areas of strength, HR can focus on leveraging these to achieve strategic objectives. Conversely, by recognizing weaknesses, HR can develop targeted training and development programs to address gaps and improve overall performance.

Utilizing Indirect Tactics

Sun Tzu states that indirect tactics, when efficiently applied, are inexhaustible. In HR, this principle can be applied through innovative and creative approaches to problem-solving and employee engagement. Indirect tactics in HR might include fostering a culture of continuous learning, implementing flexible work arrangements, and promoting a positive work-life balance.

These tactics can help to maintain high levels of employee motivation and engagement, which are critical for long-term organizational success. By continuously evolving and adapting these tactics, HR can ensure that they remain effective and relevant in a changing business environment.

IV. Strategic Energy Management

Combining Direct and Indirect Methods

Sun Tzu explains that direct and indirect methods lead to an endless series of maneuvers, much like musical notes, colors, and tastes combine to create infinite variations. In HR, combining direct and indirect methods can create a dynamic and adaptable approach to managing the workforce.

For instance, direct methods such as setting clear performance targets can be complemented by indirect methods like offering professional development opportunities and recognizing achievements. This combination helps to create a motivating environment where employees are clear about their goals and feel supported in achieving them.

Momentum and Timing

Sun Tzu likens the onset of troops to the rush of a torrent and the quality of decision-making to the swoop of a falcon. In HR, this translates to the importance of momentum and timing in implementing strategies and initiatives. HR must be adept at recognizing the right moments to introduce changes, launch new programs, and address issues.

Timing is critical for gaining buy-in from employees and ensuring the smooth implementation of initiatives. For example, introducing a new performance management system at the beginning of a fiscal year might be more effective than doing so in the middle of a busy season. HR must also maintain momentum by following through on initiatives and ensuring that they are fully integrated into the organizational culture.

V. Maintaining Order Amidst Change

Simulated Disorder and Hidden Order

Sun Tzu discusses the concept of simulated disorder to conceal true intentions. In HR, this principle can be applied to managing change and uncertainty. Change often brings a sense of disorder, but effective HR management ensures that there is underlying order and purpose.

HR can achieve this by having a clear change management plan that includes communication strategies, employee involvement, and support systems. By providing a structured approach to change, HR can help employees navigate transitions smoothly and maintain productivity and morale.

Courage and Strength

Sun Tzu notes that simulated fear postulates courage, and simulated weakness postulates strength. In HR, this can be interpreted as the importance of building resilience and confidence within the workforce. HR should focus on developing a culture where employees feel empowered to take risks, innovate, and overcome challenges.

This can be achieved through leadership development programs, mentoring, and creating opportunities for employees to take on new responsibilities and projects. By fostering a supportive environment, HR can help employees build the courage and strength needed to thrive in a competitive and rapidly changing business landscape.

VI. Maximizing Combined Energy

Utilizing Combined Energy

Sun Tzu emphasizes the importance of combined energy, likening it to the momentum of rolling logs or stones. In HR, this means harnessing the collective energy and talents of the workforce to achieve organizational goals.

HR can maximize combined energy by promoting teamwork and collaboration. This involves creating opportunities for cross-functional projects, encouraging knowledge sharing, and fostering a collaborative culture. By leveraging the diverse skills and perspectives of the workforce, HR can drive innovation and improve overall performance.

Strategic Resource Allocation

Effective utilization of combined energy also requires strategic resource allocation. HR must ensure that resources are directed towards initiatives that have the greatest potential for impact. This involves prioritizing projects, aligning resources with strategic objectives, and continuously monitoring and adjusting allocations based on changing needs and priorities.

VII. Practical Applications in HR

1. Effective Team Management

Sun Tzu's principle that controlling a large force is the same as controlling a small one, by merely dividing their numbers, is directly applicable to effective team management in HR. Managing large teams requires breaking them down into smaller, manageable units, each with clear roles and responsibilities. This ensures that every team member understands their part in the larger strategy, fostering a sense of accountability and purpose.

HR can implement this by establishing clear hierarchies and communication channels within teams. For example, large departments can be subdivided into smaller teams, each led by a team leader who reports to a higher management level. Regular meetings and well-defined reporting structures ensure that information flows smoothly, and everyone remains aligned with organizational goals. This approach mirrors Sun Tzu's strategy of using signs and signals to coordinate large armies, ensuring that even in the face of challenges, the organization remains cohesive and resilient.

2. Strategic Use of Direct and Indirect Methods

Sun Tzu's emphasis on using both direct and indirect methods to secure victory can be applied to HR strategies for achieving organizational objectives. Direct methods involve straightforward approaches such as implementing new policies or conducting training sessions. Indirect methods might include fostering a culture of continuous improvement and innovation, where employees are encouraged to develop new solutions to ongoing challenges.

For instance, while direct methods like formal training programs are essential for skill development, indirect methods such as mentoring, and peer-to-peer learning can significantly enhance these efforts. Encouraging a culture where employees share knowledge, and best practices can lead to more innovative and sustainable solutions. This dual approach ensures that HR initiatives are robust and adaptable, akin to Sun Tzu's strategy of combining direct and indirect tactics to create an inexhaustible array of maneuvers.

3. Harnessing Combined Energy for Organizational Momentum

Sun Tzu's analogy of combined energy, where individual efforts contribute to a powerful collective force, is crucial for HR in driving organizational momentum. By leveraging the strengths and skills of various team members, HR can create a synergistic environment where the whole is greater than the sum of its parts.

HR can foster this combined energy by implementing collaborative projects that require diverse skill sets. Cross-functional teams working on strategic initiatives can bring together different perspectives and expertise, leading to more comprehensive and innovative outcomes. Encouraging collaboration through team-building activities and collaborative tools ensures that employees feel connected and motivated. This collective energy, much like the momentum of rolling logs or stones described by Sun Tzu, can drive significant organizational progress and resilience.

4. Adapting to Changing Conditions

Sun Tzu's insights into the use of energy and decision-making under changing conditions are relevant to HR's role in navigating organizational dynamics. The ability to adapt quickly to changing circumstances, while maintaining a sense of order amid apparent chaos, is crucial for HR.

HR can achieve this by cultivating a flexible and responsive organizational culture. This involves training employees to handle uncertainty and change effectively and implementing agile methodologies in project management. For example, HR can promote an agile mindset by encouraging iterative processes and continuous feedback loops, allowing teams to adapt quickly to new information or shifting priorities. This adaptability ensures that the organization can navigate turbulent times without losing momentum, much like a falcon's well-timed swoop, striking decisively and effectively.

5. Utilizing Tactical Deception and Strategic Planning

Sun Tzu's concept of using deception to maintain an advantage can be applied to HR's strategic planning and execution. By strategically managing perceptions and expectations, HR can steer the organization towards its goals while mitigating risks and overcoming obstacles.

HR can use strategic planning tools to anticipate challenges and develop contingency plans. This might involve scenario planning, where HR prepares for various potential future scenarios, ensuring the organization is ready to respond effectively. Additionally, HR can use change management techniques to guide employees through transitions smoothly, addressing concerns proactively to maintain morale and productivity. By managing perceptions and maintaining strategic flexibility, HR can lead the organization through complex changes, much like Sun Tzu's skilled general who uses tactical deception to outmaneuver the enemy.

In summary, applying Sun Tzu's principles of energy in HR involves effective team management, strategic use of direct and indirect methods, harnessing combined energy, adapting to changing conditions, and utilizing tactical deception and strategic planning. By integrating these principles, HR can enhance organizational resilience, drive collective success, and maintain a competitive edge in a dynamic business environment.

VIII. Conclusion

Sun Tzu's principles of energy offer valuable insights for HR professionals seeking to optimize their strategies and operations. By harnessing collective energy, leveraging strengths and weaknesses, and combining direct and indirect methods, HR can create a dynamic and responsive work environment. Strategic energy management, effective utilization of combined energy, and maintaining order amidst change are critical for achieving organizational success. By applying these principles, HR can navigate the complexities of the modern workforce and drive organizational success.

Effective HR management involves a balance of clear structure, innovative tactics, and strategic resource allocation. By fostering a positive organizational culture, investing in talent development, and implementing robust performance management systems, HR can harness the collective energy of the workforce to achieve strategic objectives. Sun Tzu's principles provide a timeless framework for HR professionals to navigate the challenges and opportunities of today's dynamic business environment.

VI. APPLYING SUN TZU'S "WEAK POINTS AND STRONG" TO HR

I. Introduction

Effective human resources (HR) management is vital for any organization's success and sustainability. Sun Tzu's "The Art of War" offers timeless principles that can be applied to modern HR practices, especially in understanding and leveraging the weak and strong points within an organization. This essay explores how the concepts from Sun Tzu's chapter "Weak Points and Strong" can guide HR professionals in optimizing their strategies and operations to enhance organizational resilience and performance.

II. Proactive Positioning

Being First in the Field

Sun Tzu emphasizes the advantage of being first in the field and awaiting the enemy, thereby staying fresh for the fight. In HR, this translates to proactive planning and positioning. HR should anticipate market trends, workforce needs, and potential challenges to position the organization advantageously.

By conducting regular workforce planning and analysis, HR can predict future talent needs and develop strategies to meet them. This involves identifying critical roles, understanding skill gaps, and creating a talent pipeline to ensure the organization is prepared for future demands. Proactive positioning helps HR stay ahead of competitors in attracting and retaining top talent.

Imposing Will and Maintaining Control

The clever combatant imposes his will on the enemy and does not allow the enemy's will to be imposed on him. In HR, this principle can be applied by maintaining control over organizational culture and employee engagement. HR should shape the work environment and organizational culture in a way that aligns with the company's strategic goals.

This can be achieved through clear communication of organizational values, consistent reinforcement of desired behaviors, and creating a supportive and inclusive workplace. By taking charge of the organizational culture, HR can influence employee behavior and attitudes, leading to higher engagement and productivity.

III. Strategic Advantages and Harassment

Holding Out Advantages

Sun Tzu advises holding out advantages to cause the enemy to approach voluntarily. In HR, this means creating an attractive employer brand and offering incentives that draw top talent. This can include competitive compensation packages, career development opportunities, and a positive work environment.

By highlighting these advantages, HR can attract high-quality candidates who are eager to join the organization. Additionally, offering flexible work arrangements, wellness programs, and recognition schemes can enhance the organization's appeal and retain existing employees.

Harassing the Enemy

Sun Tzu also discusses the strategy of harassing the enemy to disrupt their comfort. In HR, this can be interpreted as addressing complacency within the workforce and encouraging continuous improvement. HR should implement performance management systems that set high standards and provide regular feedback.

By setting challenging goals and recognizing achievements, HR can motivate employees to strive for excellence. Additionally, offering opportunities for upskilling and professional growth can prevent complacency and foster a culture of continuous learning and improvement.

IV. Targeting Weak Points and Concealing Strengths

Attacking Undefended Positions

Sun Tzu states that success in attacks comes from targeting weak points. In HR, this involves identifying and addressing vulnerabilities within the organization. HR should conduct regular assessments to identify areas of weakness, such as skill gaps, low engagement levels, or high turnover rates.

Once identified, HR can implement targeted interventions to strengthen these areas. This might include training programs to address skill gaps, engagement initiatives to boost morale, or retention strategies to reduce turnover. By focusing on weak points, HR can enhance overall organizational resilience.

Concealing Strengths and Maintaining Secrecy

Sun Tzu highlights the importance of concealing one's strengths and maintaining secrecy. In HR, this principle can be applied by protecting sensitive information and maintaining confidentiality. This includes safeguarding employee data, strategic plans, and proprietary information.

HR should implement robust data protection policies and ensure that all employees understand the importance of confidentiality. Additionally, HR should be strategic in communicating organizational strengths, revealing them selectively to gain competitive advantage without compromising security.

V. Flexibility and Adaptability

Adapting to Circumstances

Sun Tzu explains that military tactics, like water, should be adaptable to the terrain. In HR, this principle underscores the importance of flexibility and adaptability. HR should be prepared to adjust strategies in response to changing business environments, market conditions, and workforce dynamics.

This involves staying informed about industry trends, technological advancements, and regulatory changes. HR should regularly review and update policies, procedures, and practices to ensure they remain relevant and effective. By being adaptable, HR can respond swiftly to challenges and capitalize on new opportunities.

Avoiding Predictability

Sun Tzu advises against repeating tactics that have previously succeeded. In HR, this means avoiding a one-size-fits-all approach and instead tailoring strategies to specific circumstances. HR should continuously innovate and customize their approaches based on the unique needs of different departments, teams, and individuals.

For example, recruitment strategies might vary based on the role being filled, the skills required, and the current market conditions. Similarly, employee engagement initiatives should be tailored to address the specific preferences and motivations of different employee groups. By avoiding predictability, HR can remain agile and responsive.

VI. Concentrating Strength and Dividing the Enemy

Concentrating Efforts

Sun Tzu emphasizes the power of concentrated force. In HR, this principle can be applied by focusing resources and efforts on key strategic priorities. HR should identify the most critical initiatives that will drive organizational success and allocate resources accordingly.

This might involve prioritizing leadership development

programs, investing in advanced HR technologies, or focusing on diversity and inclusion initiatives. By concentrating efforts on high-impact areas, HR can maximize their contribution to organizational performance.

Creating Division in the Opposition

Sun Tzu advises creating division within the enemy ranks. In HR, this can be interpreted as understanding and leveraging the competition's weaknesses. HR should conduct competitive intelligence to identify areas where competitors are vulnerable and develop strategies to exploit these weaknesses.

This might involve identifying gaps in competitors' employee value propositions and highlighting the unique benefits offered by your organization. Additionally, HR can monitor competitors' recruitment strategies and adapt their own approaches to attract top talent from the same talent pool.

VII. Tactical Deception and Subtlety

Simulated Disorder and Concealed Intentions

Sun Tzu discusses the value of simulated disorder and concealing true intentions. In HR, this principle can be applied to managing organizational change and uncertainty. Change initiatives often create a sense of disorder, but HR should ensure that there is a clear plan and structure behind the changes.

By managing change effectively, HR can guide the organization through transitions smoothly. This involves clear communication, employee involvement, and providing support throughout the change process. Concealing the true extent of changes until they are finalized can prevent resistance and ensure a smoother implementation.

Subtle and Indirect Tactics

Sun Tzu highlights the importance of subtle and indirect tactics. In HR, this can be applied through strategic interventions that influence behavior and outcomes without direct confrontation.

For example, HR can use incentives and recognition to encourage desired behaviors rather than imposing strict rules.

Similarly, HR can influence organizational culture through subtle cues such as the physical workspace design, communication style, and leadership behaviors. By using indirect tactics, HR can shape the work environment and employee behavior in a positive and effective manner.

VIII. Practical Applications in HR

1. Strategic Workforce Allocation

Sun Tzu's principle that those who arrive first in the field will be fresh for battle highlights the importance of strategic workforce allocation in HR. Organizations that proactively manage their human resources can ensure their teams are well-prepared and positioned to handle challenges. This involves planning and deploying employees where they can be most effective, rather than reacting to crises as they arise.

HR can achieve this by conducting regular skills assessments and workforce planning sessions to identify areas of strength and weakness. By understanding the capabilities and limitations of their workforce, HR can allocate resources more effectively, ensuring that the right people are in the right roles at the right time. This proactive approach allows organizations to maintain high performance levels and quickly respond to new opportunities or threats. For instance, if a company anticipates a surge in demand for a particular product, it can preemptively staff and train employees in relevant departments, ensuring they are ready to meet the increased workload.

2. Leveraging Competitive Intelligence

Sun Tzu's advice to impose one's will on the enemy while avoiding the imposition of the enemy's will underscores the importance of leveraging competitive intelligence in HR. By understanding the strategies and tactics of competitors, HR can develop initiatives that position the organization advantageously in the market.

HR can use competitive intelligence to benchmark against industry standards, identify best practices, and anticipate market trends. This involves gathering data on competitor hiring practices, employee benefits, and organizational culture. By understanding what makes competitors successful, HR can implement similar strategies or develop unique approaches that provide a competitive edge. For example, if a competitor is known for its innovative training programs, HR can enhance its own development initiatives to attract and retain top talent. Additionally, by monitoring competitor activities, HR can anticipate potential threats and adjust strategies, accordingly, ensuring the organization remains resilient and adaptive.

3. Identifying and Exploiting Organizational Strengths

Sun Tzu's concept of attacking weak points while defending strong ones can be directly applied to identifying and exploiting organizational strengths. HR should focus on leveraging the unique strengths of the organization and its employees to achieve competitive advantage.

This involves conducting a thorough analysis of the organization's core competencies and aligning HR strategies to support these strengths. For instance, if a company excels in customer service, HR should prioritize recruiting and training employees who can uphold and enhance this reputation. By investing in areas where the organization is already strong, HR can amplify these strengths and create a distinct market advantage. Conversely, HR should also identify areas of weakness and develop strategies to address them, whether through targeted training programs, process improvements, or strategic hiring.

4. Flexible and Adaptive Strategies

Sun Tzu's teachings on the fluidity of water and the importance of adapting tactics to the situation are highly relevant to

HR's approach to organizational strategy. In a rapidly changing business environment, flexibility and adaptability are key to sustaining success.

HR should cultivate a culture of continuous improvement and agility, encouraging employees to embrace change and innovate. This can be achieved through regular training and development programs that emphasize adaptive skills and resilience. Additionally, HR should implement flexible policies and practices that allow the organization to quickly pivot in response to market changes. For example, offering flexible work arrangements can help attract and retain talent in a competitive job market, while also enabling the organization to scale operations up or down as needed.

By regularly reviewing and adjusting HR strategies based on feedback and changing conditions, the organization can remain nimble and responsive. This approach aligns with Sun Tzu's principle of not repeating tactics that have worked in the past, but instead, adapting to the infinite variety of circumstances. HR can lead the way in fostering a dynamic and resilient organizational culture that thrives in the face of uncertainty.

5. Ensuring Effective Communication and Coordination

Sun Tzu's emphasis on the importance of coordination and keeping the enemy in a state of confusion can be applied to ensuring effective communication and coordination within the organization. Clear communication and coordinated efforts are essential for maintaining organizational cohesion and achieving strategic goals.

HR should implement robust communication channels that facilitate information flow across all levels of the organization. This includes regular updates, open forums for feedback, and transparent decision-making processes. Effective communication ensures that employees are well-informed and aligned with the organization's objectives, reducing confusion and increasing engagement. Additionally, HR can use team-building activities and collaborative projects to foster a sense of unity and cooperation among employees.

By maintaining strong communication and coordination, HR can help the organization navigate challenges smoothly and capitalize on opportunities. This approach mirrors Sun Tzu's strategy of maintaining concentrated and unified forces while causing the enemy to be divided and scattered. In the organizational context, this means keeping employees focused and aligned, enabling the organization to move forward cohesively and effectively.

IX. Conclusion

Sun Tzu's principles of weak points and strong offer valuable insights for HR professionals seeking to optimize their strategies and operations. By proactively positioning the organization, leveraging strategic advantages, and targeting weak points, HR can enhance organizational resilience and performance. Effective HR management involves a balance of direct and indirect tactics, strategic flexibility, and the ability to concentrate efforts on key priorities. By applying these principles, HR can navigate the complexities of the modern workforce and drive organizational success.

In conclusion, Sun Tzu's principles provide a timeless framework for HR professionals to enhance their strategic capabilities. By anticipating challenges, leveraging strengths, and remaining adaptable, HR can create a dynamic and responsive work environment. This strategic approach ensures that the organization is well-prepared to meet future demands and achieve long-term success.

VII APPLYING SUN TZU'S "MANEUVERING" TO HR

I. Introduction

Effective human resources (HR) management is critical for any organization's success. Sun Tzu's "The Art of War" offers timeless principles that can be applied to modern HR practices, especially in the context of maneuvering and strategy. This essay explores how the concepts from Sun Tzu's chapter "Maneuvering" can guide HR professionals in optimizing their strategies and operations to enhance organizational resilience and performance.

II. Command and Harmonization

Receiving Commands and Blending Forces

Sun Tzu begins by stating that in war, the general receives his commands from the sovereign and must blend and harmonize the different elements of his army before pitching camp. In HR, this principle emphasizes the importance of aligning HR initiatives with the organization's strategic goals set by senior leadership. HR must understand the broader business objectives and ensure that HR strategies support these goals.

To blend and harmonize the workforce, HR should focus

on building a cohesive organizational culture that unites employees under a shared vision. This involves fostering communication, collaboration, and mutual respect among different departments and teams. HR can achieve this through team-building activities, cross-functional projects, and regular communication of the company's mission and values.

III. Tactical Maneuvering

Turning Misfortune into Gain

Sun Tzu highlights the difficulty of tactical maneuvering, which involves turning the devious into the direct and misfortune into gain. In HR, this can be interpreted as the ability to navigate complex challenges and turn potential setbacks into opportunities for growth and improvement.

For example, during times of organizational change or crisis, HR must be adept at managing transitions smoothly. This involves clear communication, providing support and resources to employees, and maintaining a positive organizational culture. By doing so, HR can help the organization emerge stronger from challenges, turning potential misfortune into strategic advantages.

IV. Strategic Deviation and Rapid Maneuvering

The Art of Deviation

Sun Tzu discusses the artifice of deviation, such as taking a circuitous route to reach a goal before the enemy. In HR, this principle can be applied through strategic planning and flexibility. HR should be prepared to adapt their strategies and take unconventional approaches to achieve their objectives.

This might involve exploring new recruitment channels, adopting innovative training methods, or implementing flexible work arrangements. By being willing to deviate from traditional methods, HR can find more effective solutions and gain a competitive edge.

Rapid Maneuvering

Maneuvering with an army is advantageous, but it is dangerous with an undisciplined multitude. In HR, this underscores the importance of having a well-trained and cohesive team capable of rapid response. HR should invest in training and development to ensure that employees have the skills and knowledge needed to adapt quickly to changing circumstances.

HR should also establish clear processes and protocols for responding to different scenarios, such as sudden market changes, technological advancements, or shifts in workforce demographics. By being prepared and disciplined, HR can maneuver the organization swiftly and effectively.

V. Resource Management

Avoiding Overextension

Sun Tzu warns against overextending resources, such as making forced marches without adequate supplies. In HR, this principle can be applied to managing organizational resources effectively. HR must ensure that initiatives are well-planned and supported by adequate resources, including time, budget, and personnel.

For example, when launching a new training program, HR should ensure that there are sufficient trainers, materials, and time allocated for the program. Overextending resources can lead to burnout, decreased quality, and failure to achieve desired outcomes.

Maintaining Supply Lines

An army without its baggage-train, provisions, and bases of supply is lost. In HR, this highlights the importance of maintaining strong support systems for employees. HR should ensure that employees have access to necessary resources, such as training, tools, and support services, to perform their roles effectively.

This includes providing ongoing professional development

opportunities, access to health and wellness programs, and ensuring that employees have the technology and tools needed to work efficiently. By maintaining robust support systems, HR can enhance employee productivity and satisfaction.

VI. Strategic Alliances and Local Knowledge

Understanding the Environment

Sun Tzu emphasizes the importance of understanding the terrain, including mountains, forests, pitfalls, and precipices. In HR, this principle translates to understanding the organizational landscape and external environment. HR must be aware of industry trends, regulatory changes, and competitive dynamics that impact the organization.

HR can achieve this by conducting regular market research, staying informed about industry best practices, and building relationships with industry peers and experts. This knowledge enables HR to make informed decisions and develop strategies that are aligned with the external environment.

Utilizing Local Guides

Sun Tzu advises using local guides to turn natural advantages to account. In HR, this can be interpreted as leveraging internal expertise and engaging employees in decision-making processes. HR should involve employees in developing and implementing HR initiatives to ensure that they are relevant and effective.

This can be achieved through employee surveys, focus groups, and feedback mechanisms that allow employees to share their insights and suggestions. By involving employees in the process, HR can harness their expertise and ensure that initiatives are well-received and successful.

VII. Flexibility and Concentration

Concentration and Division

Sun Tzu states that whether to concentrate or divide troops

must be decided by circumstances. In HR, this principle can be applied to workforce planning and resource allocation. HR must be flexible and adapt their strategies based on the specific needs of the organization.

For example, during periods of rapid growth, HR might need to concentrate resources on recruitment and onboarding to ensure that new hires are integrated smoothly. Conversely, during times of economic downturn, HR might need to focus on cost-saving measures and employee retention strategies.

Rapid and Decisive Action

Sun Tzu advises that rapidity should be like the wind and compactness like the forest. In HR, this emphasizes the importance of being agile and decisive. HR should be able to respond quickly to opportunities and challenges, making swift decisions that drive organizational success.

This can be achieved through streamlined decision-making processes, clear communication channels, and a culture that encourages innovation and quick thinking. By fostering agility, HR can ensure that the organization remains competitive and resilient.

VIII. Strategic Deception and Deliberation

Concealing Intentions

Sun Tzu highlights the importance of concealing intentions and making plans impenetrable. In HR, this principle can be applied to managing change and competitive strategy. HR should be strategic in communicating plans and initiatives, revealing information selectively to prevent resistance and gain competitive advantage.

This involves having a clear communication strategy that balances transparency with discretion. HR should share information that is necessary for employees to understand their roles and responsibilities while keeping sensitive strategic plans confidential.

Pondering and Deliberating

Sun Tzu advises pondering and deliberating before making a move. In HR, this principle emphasizes the importance of thoughtful decision-making and strategic planning. HR should take the time to analyze data, consider different options, and weigh the potential outcomes before implementing initiatives.

This can be achieved through regular strategic planning sessions, involving key stakeholders in the decision-making process, and using data analytics to inform decisions. By being deliberate and strategic, HR can make informed decisions that drive long-term success.

IX. Practical Applications in HR

1. Strategic Workforce Allocation

Sun Tzu's principle of blending and harmonizing different elements before pitching camp underscores the importance of strategic workforce allocation in HR. This involves not only assembling a capable team but also ensuring that the team operates in a cohesive and coordinated manner. HR can implement this by conducting regular skills assessments and aligning team structures to meet organizational goals effectively.

HR should focus on cross-functional team development, ensuring that teams have a mix of skills and expertise that complement each other. This can be facilitated through targeted training programs and interdepartmental projects that encourage collaboration and knowledge sharing. For instance, HR can initiate cross-training programs where employees from different departments learn each other's roles, fostering a deeper understanding of the organization and enhancing teamwork. This strategic allocation of the workforce ensures that the organization can respond swiftly and effectively to new challenges and opportunities.

2. Tactical Flexibility and Adaptation

Sun Tzu's teaching on the difficulty of tactical maneuvering and the importance of turning misfortune into gain is directly applicable to HR's need for tactical flexibility and adaptation. In a constantly evolving business environment, HR must be adept at adjusting strategies to align with changing circumstances and organizational needs.

HR can develop this flexibility by adopting agile methodologies and promoting a culture of continuous improvement. This involves encouraging feedback from employees and being open to iterative changes in processes and policies. For example, HR can implement pilot programs for new initiatives, gathering data and feedback before a full-scale rollout. This allows for adjustments and improvements based on real-world performance. By staying flexible and responsive, HR can ensure that the organization remains resilient and competitive, adapting to new challenges as they arise.

3. Efficient Resource Management

Sun Tzu's advice on avoiding overextension, as demonstrated by the consequences of forced marches, highlights the necessity of efficient resource management in HR. Overworking employees can lead to burnout and diminished productivity, much like overextending an army leads to exhaustion.

HR should regularly monitor employee workloads and ensure that resources are distributed efficiently to prevent burnout. This can be achieved by implementing workload management tools and promoting a healthy work-life balance. For instance, HR can use software to track project progress and resource allocation, ensuring that no single employee or team is overwhelmed. Additionally, promoting flexible working arrangements and regular breaks can help maintain productivity and employee well-being. By managing resources wisely, HR can maintain a motivated and effective workforce, like a well-managed army maintaining its strength and readiness.

4. Enhancing Organizational Agility

Sun Tzu's principle of maneuvering to take a long and circuitous route to outpace the enemy emphasizes the importance of organizational agility. HR can enhance organizational agility by developing processes that allow the organization to pivot quickly and effectively in response to changing conditions.

HR can implement agile project management techniques, such as scrum or kanban, to improve flexibility and responsiveness. These methods encourage iterative progress, regular review sessions, and quick adaptation to new information or changes in the environment. For example, in response to market shifts, HR can quickly reassign roles and responsibilities or initiate new training programs to equip employees with necessary skills. This agility ensures that the organization can stay ahead of competitors and capitalize on emerging opportunities.

5. Leveraging Competitive Intelligence

Sun Tzu's strategy of imposing one's will on the enemy while avoiding the imposition of the enemy's will highlights the importance of leveraging competitive intelligence in HR. By understanding the strategies and practices of competitors, HR can develop initiatives that give the organization a strategic advantage.

HR can conduct regular market and competitor analyses to identify trends and best practices in the industry. This information can inform strategic decisions on policy development, training programs, and employee benefits. For example, if competitors are successfully implementing remote work policies, HR can evaluate and adopt similar practices to attract and retain top talent. Additionally, understanding competitor weaknesses allows HR to develop strategies that exploit these gaps, positioning the organization more favorably in the market.

6. Effective Communication and Coordination

Sun Tzu's emphasis on the use of gongs, drums, banners, and flags to coordinate large masses highlights the critical role of effective communication and coordination in HR. Clear and consistent communication ensures that all employees are aligned with organizational goals and can respond effectively to changes.

HR should establish robust communication channels and practices to ensure that information flows seamlessly throughout the organization. This includes regular updates, transparent decision-making processes, and platforms for feedback and discussion. For instance, HR can use internal communication tools such as intranets, newsletters, and team collaboration platforms to keep employees informed and engaged. Additionally, HR should ensure that managers are trained in effective communication techniques to foster a cohesive and informed workforce.

By applying Sun Tzu's principles of maneuvering, HR can enhance strategic flexibility, resource management, organizational agility, competitive intelligence, and communication, ultimately driving organizational success in a dynamic business environment.

X. Conclusion

Sun Tzu's principles of maneuvering offer valuable insights for HR professionals seeking to optimize their strategies and operations. By aligning HR initiatives with organizational goals, navigating complex challenges, and leveraging strategic advantages, HR can enhance organizational resilience and performance. Effective HR management involves a balance of direct and indirect tactics, strategic flexibility, and the ability to concentrate efforts on key priorities. By applying these principles, HR can navigate the complexities of the modern workforce and drive organizational success.

In conclusion, Sun Tzu's principles provide a timeless framework for HR professionals to enhance their strategic capabilities. By anticipating challenges, leveraging strengths, and remaining adaptable, HR can create a dynamic and responsive work environment. This strategic approach ensures that the organization is well-prepared to meet future demands and achieve long-term success.

VIII APPLYING SUN TZU'S "VARIATION OF TACTICS" TO HR

I. Introduction

Effective human resources (HR) management is critical for any organization's success. Sun Tzu's "The Art of War" offers timeless principles that can be applied to modern HR practices, especially in the context of varying tactics and strategies. This essay explores how the concepts from Sun Tzu's chapter "Variation of Tactics" can guide HR professionals in optimizing their strategies and operations to enhance organizational resilience and performance.

II. Strategic Flexibility

Adapting to Different Situations

Sun Tzu begins by stating that in war, the general receives his commands from the sovereign, collects his army, and concentrates his forces. In HR, this principle emphasizes the importance of aligning HR initiatives with the organization's strategic goals set by senior leadership. HR must understand the broader business objectives and ensure that HR strategies support these goals.

When in difficult situations, HR must be flexible and adaptable. This involves avoiding rigid adherence to plans when circumstances change. For instance, during an economic downturn, HR might need to shift focus from hiring to retaining existing talent and managing costs effectively. Flexibility allows HR to navigate challenges and capitalize on opportunities as they arise.

Joining Hands with Allies

In situations where high roads intersect, Sun Tzu advises joining hands with allies. In HR, this principle can be applied to building strong partnerships both within and outside the organization. Internally, HR should collaborate with other departments such as finance, marketing, and operations to ensure alignment and coherence in strategic initiatives.

Externally, HR can form alliances with educational institutions, industry associations, and other organizations to enhance recruitment, training, and development efforts. These partnerships can provide access to a broader talent pool, up-to-date industry knowledge, and valuable resources.

III. Strategic Decision-Making

Knowing What to Avoid

Sun Tzu mentions roads which must not be followed, armies which must not be attacked, and towns which must not be besieged. In HR, this principle underscores the importance of strategic decision-making and knowing when to avoid certain actions. For example, HR should be cautious about pursuing aggressive cost-cutting measures that could harm employee morale and productivity in the long term.

Similarly, HR should avoid implementing one-size-fits-all policies that may not be suitable for all departments or employee groups. By carefully considering the potential consequences of their actions, HR can make more informed decisions that support the overall health and success of the organization.

Blending Advantages and Disadvantages

Sun Tzu emphasizes the need to blend considerations of

advantage and disadvantage in the wise leader's plans. In HR, this principle can be applied through strategic planning that balances the potential benefits and risks of different initiatives. For example, when implementing a new HR technology system, HR should weigh the advantages of improved efficiency and data accuracy against the potential risks of employee resistance and implementation costs.

By conducting thorough cost-benefit analyses and risk assessments, HR can develop strategies that maximize benefits while mitigating potential downsides. This balanced approach ensures that HR initiatives are both effective and sustainable.

IV. Proactive Preparedness

Relying on Readiness

Sun Tzu teaches us to rely not on the likelihood of the enemy's not coming, but on our own readiness to receive him. In HR, this principle can be applied to proactive preparedness and risk management. HR should not rely on the assumption that challenges will not arise but should instead be prepared to address them effectively when they do.

This involves developing contingency plans for various scenarios, such as economic downturns, technological disruptions, or workforce changes. HR should conduct regular risk assessments and update contingency plans to ensure that the organization is well-prepared to handle unexpected events.

Making Positions Unassailable

Sun Tzu advises making our position unassailable rather than relying on the enemy not attacking. In HR, this means creating robust systems and processes that ensure organizational stability and resilience. This can include implementing comprehensive HR policies, establishing clear performance metrics, and maintaining strong employee support systems.

For example, HR can implement robust data security

measures to protect sensitive employee information and ensure compliance with regulations. By making their position unassailable, HR can safeguard the organization against potential threats and disruptions.

V. Avoiding Dangerous Faults

Recognizing Dangerous Faults

Sun Tzu identifies five dangerous faults that may affect a general: recklessness, cowardice, a hasty temper, a delicate sense of honor, and over-solicitude for his men. In HR, these faults can manifest in various ways and negatively impact the effectiveness of HR management.

Recklessness in HR might involve making hasty decisions without fully considering the consequences, such as implementing drastic cost-cutting measures that harm employee morale. Cowardice might be reflected in a reluctance to address difficult issues or make necessary changes. A hasty temper could lead to poor conflict resolution and strained relationships with employees. A delicate sense of honor might cause HR to prioritize image over substance, while over-solicitude for employees could lead to an overly paternalistic approach that stifles autonomy and innovation.

Meditating on Faults

Sun Tzu advises that the cause of an army's overthrow can be found among these dangerous faults. In HR, this means that HR professionals should regularly reflect on their own practices and behaviors to identify and address these faults. This involves seeking feedback from colleagues and employees, engaging in continuous professional development, and maintaining a mindset of self-awareness and improvement.

By recognizing and addressing these faults, HR can enhance their effectiveness and contribute more positively to the organization's success.

VI. Practical Applications in HR

Change Management

Effective change management is a critical area where Sun Tzu's principles can be applied. HR must be adept at managing transitions and guiding the organization through periods of change. This involves clear communication, providing support and resources to employees, and maintaining a positive organizational culture.

HR should develop comprehensive change management plans that include stakeholder analysis, communication strategies, training programs, and support mechanisms. By managing change effectively, HR can help the organization adapt to new conditions and achieve desired outcomes.

Employee Development

Employee development is another area where Sun Tzu's principles can be effectively applied. HR should implement development programs that address the needs of the organization and its employees. This involves providing continuous learning opportunities, mentorship programs, and career development pathways.

HR should also focus on developing leadership capabilities within the organization. This can be achieved through leadership development programs, succession planning, and coaching. By investing in employee development, HR can build a strong and resilient workforce capable of adapting to future challenges.

Diversity and Inclusion

Diversity and inclusion are critical areas where Sun Tzu's principles can be applied. HR should create an inclusive work environment that values diversity and promotes equal opportunities for all employees. This involves implementing policies and practices that support diversity and inclusion, such as bias training, inclusive hiring practices, and employee resource groups.

HR should also regularly assess the organization's diversity and inclusion efforts to identify areas for improvement and develop strategies to address them. By promoting diversity and inclusion, HR can enhance organizational performance and create a positive work environment.

VII. Conclusion

Sun Tzu's principles of variation of tactics offer valuable insights for HR professionals seeking to optimize their strategies and operations. By being flexible and adaptable, forming strategic alliances, making informed decisions, and being proactively prepared, HR can enhance organizational resilience and performance. Effective HR management involves balancing direct and indirect tactics, recognizing and addressing dangerous faults, and investing in critical areas such as change management, employee development, and diversity and inclusion. By applying these principles, HR can navigate the complexities of the modern workforce and drive organizational success.

In conclusion, Sun Tzu's principles provide a timeless framework for HR professionals to enhance their strategic capabilities. By anticipating challenges, leveraging strengths, and remaining adaptable, HR can create a dynamic and responsive work environment. This strategic approach ensures that the organization is well-prepared to meet future demands and achieve long-term success.

IX APPLYING SUN TZU'S "THE ARMY ON THE MARCH" TO HR

I. Introduction

Effective human resources (HR) management is critical for any organization's success. Sun Tzu's "The Art of War" offers timeless principles that can be applied to modern HR practices, especially in the context of managing resources, navigating challenges, and making strategic decisions. This essay explores how the concepts from Sun Tzu's chapter "The Army on the March" can guide HR professionals in optimizing their strategies and operations to enhance organizational resilience and performance.

II. Strategic Positioning

Encamping and Observing Signs

Sun Tzu begins by discussing the importance of encamping the army and observing signs of the enemy. In HR, this principle can be applied to understanding and monitoring the organizational environment. HR must be vigilant in observing internal and external signals that could impact the organization, such as employee morale, market trends, and competitive actions.

By staying attuned to these signals, HR can anticipate potential challenges and opportunities, allowing the organization to position itself advantageously. This involves conducting regular employee surveys, market analysis, and competitive intelligence to gather relevant data and insights.

Choosing Strategic Positions

Sun Tzu advises camping in high places facing the sun and avoiding climbing heights to fight. In HR, this principle emphasizes the importance of choosing strategic positions and leveraging natural advantages. HR should focus on creating a work environment that maximizes employee well-being and productivity.

For instance, ensuring that workspaces are well-lit, ergonomically designed, and conducive to collaboration can enhance employee satisfaction and efficiency. Additionally, HR should implement policies and practices that promote work-life balance and mental health, creating a supportive and positive work environment.

III. Navigating Challenges

Crossing Rivers and Navigating Difficult Terrain

Sun Tzu provides guidance on how to navigate difficult terrain, such as rivers and salt marshes, advising against meeting the enemy in mid-stream and emphasizing the importance of moving quickly through salt marshes. In HR, this principle can be applied to managing transitions and navigating challenging situations.

HR must be strategic in managing transitions, such as organizational restructuring, mergers, or technology implementations. This involves clear communication, providing necessary resources and support, and ensuring that employees are prepared and equipped to handle changes. By moving quickly and decisively, HR can minimize disruptions and maintain organizational stability.

Leveraging Natural Advantages

Sun Tzu advises occupying the sunny side of hills and utilizing the natural advantages of the ground. In HR, this principle can be applied to leveraging the strengths and resources available within the organization. HR should identify and capitalize on the unique strengths of the workforce, such as specialized skills, diverse perspectives, and innovative capabilities.

This involves creating opportunities for employees to showcase their talents, encouraging collaboration and innovation, and recognizing and rewarding contributions. By leveraging the natural strengths of the workforce, HR can enhance organizational performance and drive success.

IV. Risk Management

Avoiding Dangerous Situations

Sun Tzu highlights the importance of avoiding dangerous terrain and moving quickly away from areas with natural hazards. In HR, this principle can be applied to risk management and crisis preparedness. HR must identify potential risks and develop strategies to mitigate them.

This involves conducting regular risk assessments, developing contingency plans, and ensuring that the organization is prepared to respond to emergencies. By proactively managing risks, HR can protect the organization and its employees from potential harm.

Strategic Waiting

Sun Tzu advises waiting until a river subsides before crossing it and avoiding fighting on precarious terrain. In HR, this principle can be applied to strategic waiting and timing. HR must be patient and strategic in implementing initiatives, ensuring that the timing is right for maximum impact.

For example, HR might delay the launch of a new training program until after a busy season to ensure that employees can fully participate and benefit from the program. By waiting for the right moment, HR can increase the likelihood of successful implementation and positive outcomes.

V. Environmental Awareness

Monitoring and Utilizing the Environment

Sun Tzu emphasizes the importance of understanding and utilizing the environment, such as occupying high ground and avoiding quagmires. In HR, this principle can be applied to environmental awareness and sustainability. HR should promote environmentally sustainable practices within the organization.

This involves implementing policies that reduce the organization's environmental footprint, such as energy-saving initiatives, recycling programs, and sustainable procurement practices. Additionally, HR can encourage employees to adopt environmentally friendly behaviors, creating a culture of sustainability.

Using Local Guides

Sun Tzu advises using local guides to navigate unfamiliar terrain. In HR, this principle can be applied to leveraging local knowledge and expertise. HR should involve employees and local stakeholders in decision-making processes to ensure that initiatives are relevant and effective.

This involves seeking input from employees, conducting focus groups, and engaging with local communities to understand their needs and preferences. By leveraging local knowledge, HR can develop strategies that are well-informed and tailored to the specific context of the organization.

VI. Signs and Signals

Observing Signs of the Enemy

Sun Tzu discusses the importance of observing signs of the enemy, such as movement in forests, rising birds, and dust clouds. In HR, this principle can be applied to monitoring organizational health and employee behavior. HR should be vigilant in observing signs that indicate potential issues or opportunities.

This involves regularly reviewing key performance indicators (KPIs), conducting employee surveys, and monitoring feedback channels to identify trends and patterns. By staying attuned to these signs, HR can proactively address issues and capitalize on opportunities.

Interpreting Behavior

Sun Tzu emphasizes the importance of interpreting the enemy's behavior, such as humble words and increased preparations indicating an impending attack. In HR, this principle can be applied to interpreting employee behavior and organizational dynamics. HR should be skilled in understanding the underlying motivations and sentiments of employees.

This involves building strong relationships with employees, creating open channels of communication, and fostering a culture of trust and transparency. By understanding employee behavior, HR can identify potential issues early and take appropriate actions to address them.

VII. Leadership and Discipline

Balancing Humanity and Discipline

Sun Tzu advises treating soldiers with humanity but maintaining strict discipline. In HR, this principle can be applied to balancing empathy and discipline in leadership. HR leaders should demonstrate compassion and understanding while ensuring that organizational policies and standards are upheld.

This involves providing support and resources to employees, addressing their concerns, and recognizing their contributions. At the same time, HR leaders must enforce policies consistently and fairly, ensuring that employees adhere to organizational standards. By balancing humanity and discipline, HR can create a positive and productive work environment.

Enforcing Commands and Building Trust

Sun Tzu emphasizes the importance of enforcing commands and building trust. In HR, this principle can be applied to building a culture of accountability and trust. HR leaders should set clear expectations, communicate effectively, and hold employees accountable for their actions.

This involves establishing performance standards, providing regular feedback, and addressing performance issues promptly. Additionally, HR leaders should demonstrate integrity and reliability, building trust with employees through their actions and decisions. By fostering a culture of accountability and trust, HR can enhance organizational performance and employee satisfaction.

VIII. Practical Applications in HR

Health and Safety

Health and safety are a critical area where Sun Tzu's principles can be applied. HR must ensure that the workplace is safe and conducive to employee well-being. This involves implementing safety protocols, conducting regular inspections, and providing training on health and safety practices.

HR should also promote a culture of safety by encouraging employees to report hazards and near-misses and by recognizing and rewarding safe behavior. By prioritizing health and safety, HR can protect employees and enhance organizational performance.

Technology Integration

Technology integration is another area where Sun Tzu's principles can be effectively applied. HR should leverage technology to enhance efficiency, productivity, and employee engagement. This involves implementing HR information systems (HRIS), using data analytics to inform decision-making, and adopting digital tools for communication and collaboration.

HR should also ensure that employees are trained and

supported in using new technologies, providing resources and assistance as needed. By integrating technology effectively, HR can streamline processes and improve overall organizational performance.

Crisis Management

Crisis management is a critical area where Sun Tzu's principles can be applied. HR must be prepared to respond to emergencies and crises, such as natural disasters, pandemics, or cybersecurity breaches. This involves developing comprehensive crisis management plans, conducting regular drills and simulations, and ensuring that employees are trained and prepared.

HR should also establish clear communication channels and protocols for reporting and responding to crises. By being prepared and proactive, HR can protect the organization and its employees from potential harm.

Leveraging AI for Strategic Advantage

Incorporating artificial intelligence (AI) into HR practices aligns with Sun Tzu's principles of leveraging technology and resources for strategic advantage. AI can significantly enhance HR functions such as talent acquisition, performance management, and employee engagement. By automating repetitive tasks, AI frees up HR professionals to focus on strategic initiatives that drive organizational success. AI-powered tools can analyze vast amounts of data to identify trends, predict future workforce needs, and recommend actions to improve employee satisfaction and productivity. For example, AI can streamline the recruitment process by screening resumes, scheduling interviews, and even conducting initial assessments, ensuring that HR can attract and retain top talent more efficiently.

Enhancing Decision-Making with Data Analytics

Sun Tzu emphasized the importance of making informed

decisions based on thorough analysis. AI and data analytics enable HR to make more accurate and timely decisions. Predictive analytics can forecast employee turnover, identify potential skill gaps, and suggest targeted interventions to address these issues. By utilizing AI-driven insights, HR can develop more effective strategies for workforce planning, talent development, and succession planning. This data-driven approach ensures that HR decisions are aligned with organizational goals and can adapt to changing business environments.

Improving Employee Experience and Engagement

AI can also enhance the employee experience by providing personalized learning and development opportunities, offering real-time feedback, and facilitating continuous performance management. AI-driven platforms can recommend training programs based on individual career paths, helping employees develop the skills they need to advance within the organization. Moreover, AI-powered chatbots and virtual assistants can provide employees with immediate answers to their HR-related queries, improving their overall satisfaction and engagement. By leveraging AI to create a more responsive and supportive work environment, HR can foster a culture of continuous improvement and innovation.

IX. Conclusion

Sun Tzu's principles of the army on the march offer valuable insights for HR professionals seeking to optimize their strategies and operations. By understanding and monitoring the organizational environment, navigating challenges, managing risks, and balancing empathy and discipline, HR can enhance organizational resilience and performance. Effective HR management involves leveraging natural advantages, interpreting behavior, enforcing commands, and building trust. By applying these principles, HR can navigate the complexities of the modern workforce and drive organizational success.

In conclusion, Sun Tzu's principles provide a timeless framework for HR professionals to enhance their strategic capabilities. By anticipating challenges, leveraging strengths, and remaining adaptable, HR can create a dynamic and responsive work environment. This strategic approach ensures that the organization is well-prepared to meet future demands and achieve long-term success.

X APPLYING SUN TZU'S "TERRAIN" TO HR

I. Introduction

Effective human resources (HR) management is crucial for any organization's success. Sun Tzu's "The Art of War" offers timeless principles that can be applied to modern HR practices, particularly in understanding and leveraging various types of terrain, both literal and metaphorical, within an organization. This essay explores how the concepts from Sun Tzu's chapter "Terrain" can guide HR professionals in optimizing their strategies and operations to enhance organizational resilience and performance.

II. Understanding Organizational Terrain

Six Types of Terrain

Sun Tzu distinguishes six kinds of terrain: accessible ground, entangling ground, temporizing ground, narrow passes, precipitous heights, and positions at a great distance from the enemy. In HR, these terrains can be metaphorically translated into different organizational contexts and challenges that HR professionals must navigate.

- Accessible Ground: Areas within the organization that are easy to navigate and where communication flows freely. These are departments or teams that are well-integrated and function smoothly.

- Entangling Ground: Situations that are easy to enter but difficult to exit, such as complex projects or interdepartmental conflicts.
- Temporizing Ground: Scenarios where neither party gains by making the first move, such as strategic standoffs or negotiations.
- Narrow Passes: Critical junctures or bottlenecks in processes that require careful management to avoid delays or conflicts.
- Precipitous Heights: High-stakes situations or positions of strategic advantage that need to be occupied swiftly to maintain dominance.
- Distant Positions: Remote or decentralized teams and operations that pose challenges in terms of coordination and communication.

III. Navigating Accessible Ground

Proactive Occupation

Sun Tzu advises being first in occupying raised and sunny spots on accessible ground. In HR, this translates to proactively managing areas of the organization that are straightforward and well-integrated. HR should ensure that these areas are optimized for efficiency and productivity.

This can be achieved by implementing robust communication systems, providing clear guidelines and policies, and ensuring that these departments have the necessary resources and support to function effectively. By maintaining a strong presence in accessible areas, HR can foster a positive work environment and prevent issues from arising.

Guarding Supplies

Sun Tzu emphasizes the importance of guarding supply lines on accessible ground. In HR, this means ensuring that essential resources and support systems are in place and maintained. This includes providing employees with the necessary tools, training, and resources to perform their roles effectively.

HR should regularly review and update resource allocations, ensure that supplies are readily available, and address any gaps or shortages promptly. By doing so, HR can maintain operational stability and support employee productivity.

IV. Managing Entangling Ground

Strategic Engagement

Entangling ground, which can be abandoned but is hard to re-occupy, represents situations that require careful consideration before engagement. In HR, this can be related to complex projects or initiatives that have significant implications for the organization.

HR should approach these situations strategically, ensuring that thorough planning and risk assessment are conducted before committing resources. If the organization is unprepared or the risks are too high, HR should avoid engagement and seek alternative solutions. If engagement is necessary, HR should ensure that contingency plans are in place to manage potential challenges.

V. Handling Temporizing Ground

Strategic Patience

Temporizing ground is characterized by scenarios where neither side gains by making the first move. In HR, this can occur during strategic negotiations or decision-making processes where timing is critical.

HR should exercise strategic patience in these situations, avoiding hasty decisions and waiting for the opportune moment to act. This involves carefully analyzing the situation, monitoring developments, and being prepared to act when conditions are favorable. By doing so, HR can make more informed decisions and achieve better outcomes.

VI. Navigating Narrow Passes

Securing Critical Junctures

Narrow passes represent critical junctures or bottlenecks that require careful management. In HR, this can include key decision points, important projects, or high-stakes negotiations that have significant implications for the organization.

HR should ensure that these critical junctures are managed effectively by allocating adequate resources, involving the right stakeholders, and closely monitoring progress. By securing these positions, HR can prevent delays and ensure that strategic initiatives are successfully implemented.

VII. Leveraging Precipitous Heights

Occupying Strategic Positions

Precipitous heights represent positions of strategic advantage that need to be occupied swiftly to maintain dominance. In HR, this can include leadership positions, strategic initiatives, or high-impact projects that provide a competitive edge.

HR should be proactive in identifying and securing these strategic positions, ensuring that the organization is well-positioned to capitalize on opportunities. This involves identifying key talent, developing leadership capabilities, and ensuring that strategic initiatives are aligned with organizational goals.

VIII. Managing Distant Positions

Coordinating Remote Operations

Positions at a great distance from the enemy represent remote or decentralized teams and operations that pose challenges in terms of coordination and communication. In HR, this translates to managing remote workforces, global teams, or decentralized operations.

HR should implement robust communication and collaboration

tools to ensure that remote teams are well-connected and aligned with organizational objectives. This involves providing support for remote work, fostering a sense of belonging and inclusion, and ensuring that remote employees have access to the necessary resources and support.

IX. Addressing Organizational Calamities

Identifying and Mitigating Faults

Sun Tzu identifies six calamities that can affect an army: flight, insubordination, collapse, ruin, disorganization, and rout. In HR, these calamities can be translated into organizational failures that need to be identified and mitigated.

- Flight: High employee turnover due to poor management or lack of engagement.
- Insubordination: Lack of respect for authority and organizational rules, leading to chaos and inefficiency.
- Collapse: Breakdown of team cohesion and morale, resulting in poor performance and productivity.
- Ruin: Financial or reputational damage due to poor decision-making or unethical behavior.
- Disorganization: Lack of clear roles, responsibilities, and processes, leading to confusion and inefficiency.
- Rout: Complete breakdown of organizational structure and leadership, leading to failure.

HR should be vigilant in identifying these potential calamities and implementing strategies to mitigate them. This involves establishing clear roles and responsibilities, fostering a positive organizational culture, and ensuring that leadership is effective and accountable.

X. Practical Applications in HR

Health and Safety

Health and safety are a critical area where Sun Tzu's principles can be applied. HR must ensure that the workplace is safe and conducive to employee well-being. This involves implementing safety protocols, conducting regular inspections, and providing training on health and safety practices.

HR should also promote a culture of safety by encouraging employees to report hazards and near-misses and by recognizing and rewarding safe behavior. By prioritizing health and safety, HR can protect employees and enhance organizational performance.

Technology Integration

Technology integration is another area where Sun Tzu's principles can be effectively applied. HR should leverage technology to enhance efficiency, productivity, and employee engagement. This involves implementing HR information systems (HRIS), using data analytics to inform decision-making, and adopting digital tools for communication and collaboration.

HR should also ensure that employees are trained and supported in using new technologies, providing resources and assistance as needed. By integrating technology effectively, HR can streamline processes and improve overall organizational performance.

Crisis Management

Crisis management is a critical area where Sun Tzu's principles can be applied. HR must be prepared to respond to emergencies and crises, such as natural disasters, pandemics, or cybersecurity breaches. This involves developing comprehensive crisis management plans, conducting regular drills and simulations, and ensuring that employees are trained and prepared.

HR should also establish clear communication channels and protocols for reporting and responding to crises. By being prepared and proactive, HR can protect the organization and its employees from potential harm.

XI. Conclusion

Sun Tzu's principles of terrain offer valuable insights for HR professionals seeking to optimize their strategies and operations. By understanding and navigating different organizational contexts, managing risks, leveraging strategic positions, and addressing potential calamities, HR can enhance organizational resilience and performance. Effective HR management involves balancing proactive and reactive strategies, leveraging technology, and prioritizing health and safety. By applying these principles, HR can navigate the complexities of the modern workforce and drive organizational success.

In conclusion, Sun Tzu's principles provide a timeless framework for HR professionals to enhance their strategic capabilities. By anticipating challenges, leveraging strengths, and remaining adaptable, HR can create a dynamic and responsive work environment. This strategic approach ensures that the organization is well-prepared to meet future demands and achieve long-term success.

XI APPLYING SUN TZU'S "THE NINE SITUATIONS" TO HR

I. Introduction

Effective human resources (HR) management is crucial for any organization's success. Sun Tzu's "The Art of War" offers timeless principles that can be applied to modern HR practices, particularly in navigating various organizational contexts and challenges. This essay explores how the concepts from Sun Tzu's chapter "The Nine Situations" can guide HR professionals in optimizing their strategies and operations to enhance organizational resilience and performance.

II. Understanding Organizational Situations

The Nine Types of Situations

Sun Tzu distinguishes nine varieties of ground: dispersive, facile, contentious, open, intersecting highways, serious, difficult, hemmed-in, and desperate. In HR, these terrains can be metaphorically translated into different organizational contexts that HR professionals must navigate:

1. Dispersive Ground: Situations where the organization is spread thin, such as managing a dispersed workforce or multiple remote offices.
2. Facile Ground: Early stages of market entry or new project initiation, where progress is easy but limited.
3. Contentious   Ground: Highly   competitive

environments or internal conflicts where control is crucial.

4. Open Ground: Scenarios where freedom of movement and decision-making is available to both HR and employees.
5. Intersecting Highways: Key strategic points that influence multiple areas, such as critical projects or key leadership positions.
6. Serious Ground: Deeply embedded organizational initiatives or crises requiring comprehensive strategies.
7. Difficult Ground: Challenging situations such as regulatory changes, economic downturns, or significant restructurings.
8. Hemmed-In Ground: Scenarios with limited options, such as severe budget constraints or high employee turnover.
9. Desperate Ground: Critical situations requiring immediate action to avoid severe negative outcomes, such as legal issues or major PR crises.

III. Navigating Dispersive Ground

Managing a Dispersed Workforce

On dispersive ground, Sun Tzu advises not to fight. In HR, this translates to managing a dispersed workforce without creating unnecessary conflicts or stress. HR should focus on building strong communication channels and fostering a sense of unity and purpose among employees spread across different locations.

This can be achieved through regular virtual meetings, team-building activities, and clear communication of organizational goals. Providing consistent support and resources to remote workers ensures they remain engaged and productive, despite the physical distance.

IV. Halting on Facile Ground

Early-Stage Initiatives

On facile ground, Sun Tzu advises not to halt. In HR, this applies to early-stage initiatives such as new projects or market entries. HR should maintain momentum and avoid complacency to ensure these initiatives progress smoothly.

HR can achieve this by setting clear milestones, regularly reviewing progress, and addressing any obstacles promptly. By keeping the initiative moving forward, HR can capitalize on early successes and build a strong foundation for future growth.

V. Engaging on Contentious Ground

Navigating Competitive Environments

On contentious ground, Sun Tzu advises not to attack. In HR, this can be applied to highly competitive environments or internal conflicts. Instead of direct confrontation, HR should focus on strategic positioning and negotiation to gain an advantage.

This involves understanding the competitive landscape, identifying key strengths and weaknesses, and leveraging negotiation skills to resolve conflicts or secure advantageous positions. By adopting a strategic approach, HR can navigate contentious situations effectively without unnecessary confrontation.

VI. Moving Freely on Open Ground

Freedom of Movement

On open ground, Sun Tzu advises not to block the enemy's way. In HR, this translates to providing employees with the freedom to move and make decisions. HR should create an environment where employees feel empowered to take initiative and explore new opportunities.

This involves fostering a culture of trust and autonomy, encouraging innovation, and supporting employees in their professional development. By allowing freedom of movement, HR can unlock the full potential of the workforce and drive organizational success.

VII. Consolidating on Intersecting Highways

Key Strategic Points

On ground of intersecting highways, Sun Tzu advises joining hands with allies. In HR, this refers to key strategic points that influence multiple areas of the organization, such as critical projects or leadership positions. HR should build strong alliances and collaborate with other departments to ensure success.

This involves identifying key stakeholders, fostering collaboration, and ensuring that strategic initiatives are aligned with overall organizational goals. By consolidating efforts and resources, HR can maximize the impact of key strategic initiatives.

VIII. Strategizing on Serious Ground

Deeply Embedded Initiatives

On serious ground, Sun Tzu advises gathering in plunder. In HR, this translates to deeply embedded organizational initiatives or crises requiring comprehensive strategies. HR should develop detailed plans and mobilize resources to address these situations effectively.

This involves conducting thorough analysis, identifying key objectives, and implementing strategic actions to achieve desired outcomes. By taking a comprehensive approach, HR can navigate serious situations and drive organizational success.

IX. Advancing on Difficult Ground

Overcoming Challenges

On difficult ground, Sun Tzu advises keeping steadily on the march. In HR, this applies to challenging situations such as regulatory changes, economic downturns, or significant restructurings. HR should remain persistent and focused, continuously moving forward despite obstacles.

This involves maintaining a positive outlook, providing support and resources to employees, and implementing adaptive strategies to overcome challenges. By staying focused and resilient, HR can navigate difficult situations and ensure organizational stability.

X. Employing Stratagems on Hemmed-In Ground
Limited Options

On hemmed-in ground, Sun Tzu advises resorting to stratagem. In HR, this refers to scenarios with limited options, such as severe budget constraints or high employee turnover. HR should employ creative and strategic solutions to navigate these situations.

This involves thinking outside the box, leveraging available resources efficiently, and finding innovative ways to address challenges. By employing strategic thinking, HR can navigate hemmed-in situations and find pathways to success.

XI. Fighting on Desperate Ground
Critical Situations

On desperate ground, Sun Tzu advises fighting. In HR, this translates to critical situations requiring immediate action to avoid severe negative outcomes, such as legal issues or major PR crises. HR should act decisively and mobilize resources quickly to address these situations.

This involves having crisis management plans in place, ensuring clear communication, and taking swift action to mitigate risks. By acting decisively, HR can navigate desperate situations and protect the organization from severe harm.

XII. Practical Applications in HR

Compensation and Benefits

Compensation and benefits are critical areas where Sun Tzu's principles can be applied. HR must ensure that compensation structures are competitive and aligned with market standards. This involves conducting regular market analyses, reviewing compensation policies, and adjusting as needed to attract and retain top talent.

HR should also focus on providing a comprehensive benefits package that meets the diverse needs of employees. This includes health and wellness programs, retirement plans, and work-life balance initiatives. By offering competitive compensation and benefits, HR can enhance employee satisfaction and retention.

Employee Relations

Employee relations are another area where Sun Tzu's principles can be effectively applied. HR should foster positive relationships between employees and management, ensuring a harmonious and productive work environment. This involves addressing employee concerns promptly, mediating conflicts, and promoting open communication.

HR should also implement policies and practices that promote fairness and transparency, ensuring that employees feel valued and respected. By fostering positive employee relations, HR can enhance organizational culture and drive performance.

Organizational Development

Organizational development is a critical area where Sun Tzu's principles can be applied. HR should focus on developing the organization's structure, processes, and culture to support long-term success. This involves conducting organizational assessments, identifying areas for improvement, and implementing strategic initiatives to drive growth and development.

HR should also focus on leadership development, ensuring that leaders have the skills and capabilities to guide the organization effectively. This includes providing training, coaching, and mentorship programs to support leadership growth. By investing in organizational development, HR can enhance overall performance and drive success.

XIII. Conclusion

Sun Tzu's principles of the nine situations offer valuable insights for HR professionals seeking to optimize their strategies and operations. By understanding and navigating different organizational contexts, managing risks, leveraging strategic positions, and addressing potential calamities, HR can enhance organizational resilience and performance. Effective HR management involves balancing proactive and reactive strategies, leveraging technology, and prioritizing health and safety. By applying these principles, HR can navigate the complexities of the modern workforce and drive organizational success.

In conclusion, Sun Tzu's principles provide a timeless framework for HR professionals to enhance their strategic capabilities. By anticipating challenges, leveraging strengths, and remaining adaptable, HR can create a dynamic and responsive work environment. This strategic approach ensures that the organization is well-prepared to meet future demands and achieve long-term success.

XII APPLYING SUN TZU'S "THE ATTACK BY FIRE" TO HR

I. Introduction

Effective human resources (HR) management is critical for any organization's success. Sun Tzu's "The Art of War" offers timeless principles that can be applied to modern HR practices, particularly in the context of strategic interventions and crisis management. This essay explores how the concepts from Sun Tzu's chapter "The Attack by Fire" can guide HR professionals in optimizing their strategies and operations to enhance organizational resilience and performance.

II. Strategic Interventions

Types of Interventions

Sun Tzu describes five ways of attacking with fire: burning soldiers in their camp, burning stores, burning baggage-trains, burning arsenals and magazines, and hurling dropping fire among the enemy. In HR, these can be metaphorically translated into different types of strategic interventions:

1. Burning Soldiers in Their Camp: Addressing employee morale and engagement issues within their own teams and departments.
2. Burning Stores: Managing and optimizing resources such as training programs and development initiatives.

3. Burning Baggage-Trains: Streamlining administrative processes and reducing bureaucratic inefficiencies.
4. Burning Arsenals and Magazines: Ensuring that tools, technologies, and knowledge repositories are up-to-date and secure.
5. Hurling Dropping Fire: Implementing unexpected changes or innovations to disrupt complacency and stimulate progress.

Readiness for Action

Sun Tzu emphasizes the importance of having the material for raising fire ready. In HR, this translates to being prepared for strategic interventions with the necessary tools, resources, and plans in place. HR should maintain an inventory of resources, including training materials, technological tools, and a pool of skilled personnel, to deploy interventions effectively.

III. Timing and Conditions

Proper Season for Action

Sun Tzu advises that there is a proper season and specific days for making attacks with fire. In HR, this principle underscores the importance of timing and conditions for implementing strategic initiatives. HR should carefully analyze the organizational climate, market conditions, and employee readiness before launching significant changes or interventions.

For example, rolling out a new performance management system during a busy season might lead to resistance and poor adoption. Instead, HR should choose a time when employees can fully engage with the new system, ensuring a smoother transition and better outcomes.

IV. Responding to Developments

Five Possible Developments

Sun Tzu outlines five developments to consider when attacking with fire: responding immediately to internal disruptions, biding time if the enemy remains quiet, attacking at the height of the flames, attacking from outside if feasible, and positioning oneself to windward. In HR, these principles can be applied to responding to organizational changes and crises:

1. Immediate Response: When internal disruptions occur, such as employee unrest or sudden turnover, HR should act swiftly to address the issues and stabilize the situation.
2. Biding Time: If there are signs of potential issues but no immediate action from employees, HR should monitor the situation closely and be ready to intervene when necessary.
3. Height of the Flames: During peak moments of change or crisis, HR should take decisive action to manage the situation effectively.
4. External Opportunities: If there are opportunities to introduce beneficial changes from outside influences, HR should seize the moment.
5. Strategic Positioning: HR should ensure that interventions are strategically positioned to maximize their impact and align with organizational goals.

V. Intelligence and Strength

Using Fire and Water

Sun Tzu notes that using fire shows intelligence, while using water gains strength. In HR, this principle translates to using different types of interventions to address organizational challenges:

- Intelligent Interventions: Strategic changes that require careful planning and execution, such as restructuring, introducing new technologies, or revamping HR policies.
- Strength-Building Interventions: Initiatives that enhance organizational resilience and capacity, such

as leadership development programs, employee wellness initiatives, and team-building activities.

By balancing intelligent and strength-building interventions, HR can create a robust and adaptive organization.

VI. Planning and Resource Cultivation

Laying Plans and Cultivating Resources

Sun Tzu emphasizes the importance of laying plans well ahead and cultivating resources. In HR, this translates to strategic workforce planning and resource development. HR should anticipate future needs and trends, and develop plans to address them proactively.

This involves conducting regular workforce assessments, identifying skill gaps, and investing in training and development programs to build the necessary capabilities. Additionally, HR should cultivate a pipeline of talent to ensure that the organization has the right people in place to meet future challenges.

VII. Decision-Making and Caution

Strategic Decision-Making

Sun Tzu advises moving only when there is an advantage, using troops only when there is something to gain, and fighting only when the position is critical. In HR, this principle emphasizes the importance of strategic decision-making. HR should avoid making hasty decisions or implementing changes without a clear benefit.

For example, HR should conduct thorough cost-benefit analyses before implementing new initiatives, ensuring that the potential gains outweigh the risks. By making informed decisions, HR can maximize the impact of their interventions and avoid unnecessary disruptions.

Caution and Prudence

Sun Tzu highlights the importance of caution and prudence, noting that anger and vexation are transient, but the consequences of rash actions can be permanent. In HR, this translates to exercising caution in managing employee relations and organizational changes.

HR should strive to maintain a calm and measured approach, even in challenging situations. This involves clear communication, seeking input from stakeholders, and considering the long-term implications of decisions. By fostering a culture of caution and prudence, HR can protect the organization from potential pitfalls.

VIII. Practical Applications in HR

Compliance and Risk Management

Compliance and risk management are critical areas where Sun Tzu's principles can be applied. HR must ensure that the organization complies with relevant laws and regulations, and that risks are managed effectively. This involves implementing robust compliance programs, conducting regular audits, and providing training on legal and regulatory requirements.

HR should also develop risk management strategies to identify and mitigate potential risks. This includes conducting risk assessments, developing contingency plans, and ensuring that the organization is prepared to respond to emergencies.

Organizational Culture

Organizational culture is another area where Sun Tzu's principles can be effectively applied. HR should foster a positive and inclusive culture that aligns with the organization's values and goals. This involves implementing policies and practices that promote diversity, equity, and inclusion, as well as creating a supportive and engaging work environment.

HR should also focus on cultural alignment during times of change, ensuring that new initiatives and changes are consistent with the organization's values. By fostering a strong and positive culture, HR can enhance employee satisfaction and performance.

Learning and Development

Learning and development is a critical area where Sun Tzu's principles can be applied. HR should implement comprehensive training and development programs to build the skills and capabilities of employees. This involves providing ongoing learning opportunities, creating individualized development plans, and leveraging technology to enhance learning experiences.

HR should also focus on leadership development, ensuring that leaders have the skills and capabilities to guide the organization effectively. This includes providing training, coaching, and mentorship programs to support leadership growth. By investing in learning and development, HR can build a strong and resilient workforce capable of adapting to future challenges.

IX. Conclusion

Sun Tzu's principles of the attack by fire offer valuable insights for HR professionals seeking to optimize their strategies and operations. By understanding and navigating different organizational contexts, managing risks, leveraging strategic positions, and addressing potential crises, HR can enhance organizational resilience and performance. Effective HR management involves balancing proactive and reactive strategies, leveraging technology, and prioritizing health and safety. By applying these principles, HR can navigate the complexities of the modern workforce and drive organizational success.

In conclusion, Sun Tzu's principles provide a timeless framework for HR professionals to enhance their strategic capabilities. By anticipating challenges, leveraging strengths, and remaining adaptable, HR can create a dynamic and responsive work environment. This strategic approach ensures that the organization is well-prepared to meet future demands and achieve long-term success.

XIII APPLYING SUN TZU'S "THE USE OF SPIES" TO HR

I. Introduction

Effective human resources (HR) management is essential for any organization's success. Sun Tzu's "The Art of War" offers timeless principles that can be applied to modern HR practices, particularly in the context of gathering and utilizing information. This essay explores how the concepts from Sun Tzu's chapter "The Use of Spies" can guide HR professionals in optimizing their strategies and operations to enhance organizational resilience and performance.

II. The Importance of Information

The Cost of Ignorance

Sun Tzu emphasizes the heavy cost of ignorance in warfare, highlighting the strain on resources and the potential for failure. In HR, this principle underscores the importance of information gathering and analysis. Without accurate and timely information, HR cannot make informed decisions, leading to wasted resources and missed opportunities.

HR should prioritize data collection and analysis to understand employee needs, market trends, and organizational performance. This involves leveraging HR information systems (HRIS), conducting regular surveys, and maintaining open communication channels with employees and other stakeholders.

III. Foreknowledge and Intelligence

Foreknowledge as a Strategic Asset

Sun Tzu attributes the success of wise leaders to their ability to obtain foreknowledge. In HR, this translates to using predictive analytics and strategic workforce planning. By analyzing trends and patterns, HR can anticipate future needs and challenges, allowing the organization to prepare and adapt proactively.

For example, HR can use data analytics to predict turnover rates and identify factors contributing to employee attrition. By addressing these factors proactively, HR can improve retention and maintain a stable workforce.

IV. Types of "Spies" in HR

Local Spies: Internal Employee Feedback

Sun Tzu mentions local spies as inhabitants of a district who provide valuable information. In HR, this can be likened to gathering feedback from employees through surveys, focus groups, and one-on-one meetings. Internal feedback helps HR understand employee satisfaction, engagement, and areas for improvement.

Regularly conducting employee satisfaction surveys and holding feedback sessions allows HR to stay attuned to employee needs and address issues promptly. This internal intelligence is crucial for maintaining a positive work environment and enhancing overall productivity.

Inward Spies: Cross-Departmental Collaboration

Inward spies are officials of the enemy used to gather information. In HR, this principle can be applied to cross-departmental collaboration. By working closely with other departments, HR can gain insights into different areas of the organization, identify potential issues, and develop more effective strategies.

For instance, collaborating with the finance department can provide HR with a better understanding of budget constraints and financial goals, allowing for more aligned and efficient HR initiatives.

Converted Spies: Leveraging External Consultants

Converted spies are enemy agents turned to work for one's own side. In HR, this can be translated into leveraging external consultants and industry experts who provide insights and best practices. These professionals can offer a fresh perspective and help HR develop innovative solutions to complex challenges.

Engaging external consultants for strategic projects, such as organizational restructuring or leadership development, can provide HR with valuable expertise and enhance the effectiveness of their initiatives.

Doomed Spies: Controlled Information Release

Doomed spies are used to deceive the enemy by feeding them false information. In HR, this principle can be applied to controlled information release. By strategically releasing information about upcoming changes or initiatives, HR can manage employee expectations and reactions.

For example, when planning a significant organizational change, HR can release information in stages to prepare employees gradually and minimize resistance. This controlled approach helps manage the transition smoothly and maintains organizational stability.

Surviving Spies: Monitoring External Environment

Surviving spies bring back news from the enemy's camp. In HR, this involves monitoring the external environment, including market trends, competitor actions, and industry developments. By staying informed about external factors, HR can adapt strategies to remain competitive and responsive to changes.

HR should regularly review industry reports, attend

conferences, and engage with professional networks to stay updated on external trends and developments. This external intelligence is crucial for strategic planning and maintaining a competitive edge.

V. Managing Information and Intelligence

The Role of Data Analytics

Sun Tzu highlights the importance of obtaining information from various sources. In HR, data analytics plays a critical role in gathering and analyzing information. HR should invest in advanced data analytics tools to track key metrics, identify trends, and make data-driven decisions.

For instance, predictive analytics can help HR forecast workforce needs, identify potential skill gaps, and develop targeted training programs. By leveraging data analytics, HR can enhance their strategic capabilities and improve organizational performance.

Ensuring Confidentiality and Trust

Sun Tzu emphasizes the need for secrecy and trust in managing spies. In HR, maintaining confidentiality and building trust with employees is paramount. HR must handle sensitive information with care and ensure that employee data is protected.

This involves implementing robust data security measures, establishing clear policies for data handling, and fostering a culture of trust and transparency. By ensuring confidentiality, HR can build trust with employees and encourage open communication.

VI. Practical Applications in HR

Practical Applications of Sun Tzu's "The Use of Spies" in HR: Strategic Intelligence and Information Management

1. Strategic Workforce Insights

Sun Tzu's emphasis on the importance of foreknowledge and

the use of spies highlights the need for HR to gather strategic workforce insights. Just as foreknowledge is essential for a general to achieve victory, understanding employee sentiment, market conditions, and competitor strategies is crucial for HR to make informed decisions and anticipate future challenges.

HR can employ various methods to gather these insights. For example, internal surveys and feedback tools can serve as "local spies," providing valuable information about employee satisfaction and engagement. Regularly conducting exit interviews can also uncover reasons for employee turnover, offering insights into potential areas of improvement within the organization. Furthermore, HR can leverage industry reports, professional networks, and benchmarking studies to gain an understanding of market trends and competitor practices. By systematically collecting and analyzing this information, HR can develop strategies that align with organizational goals and improve overall workforce effectiveness.

Incorporating AI into this process can significantly enhance the accuracy and efficiency of gathering and analyzing strategic insights. AI-powered analytics tools can process vast amounts of data from various sources, including employee feedback, industry trends, and social media sentiment, providing HR with real-time insights. Machine learning algorithms can identify patterns and predict future workforce trends, enabling HR to proactively address potential issues and capitalize on opportunities. By using AI to augment their strategic foreknowledge, HR professionals can make more informed decisions, improve employee satisfaction, and maintain a competitive edge in the market.

2. Internal Communication and Information Sharing

Sun Tzu's discussion of using different types of spies to gather and manage information can be applied to HR's role in internal communication and information sharing. Effective communication channels are essential for ensuring that accurate and relevant information is disseminated throughout the organization, enabling informed decision-making and strategic alignment.

HR should establish robust communication networks that facilitate the flow of information between different departments and levels of the organization. This includes implementing regular updates, internal newsletters, and town hall meetings where employees can share insights and feedback. Additionally, HR can create cross-functional teams or committees that act as "inward spies," gathering and sharing knowledge from various parts of the organization. These teams can identify potential issues, foster collaboration, and ensure that all employees are aligned with the organization's strategic objectives. By maintaining effective internal communication, HR can enhance organizational cohesion and responsiveness.

3. Competitive Intelligence and Strategic Positioning

Sun Tzu's use of converted spies to gather critical information from the enemy can be likened to HR's need for competitive intelligence to inform strategic positioning. Understanding the strengths, weaknesses, and strategies of competitors is essential for HR to develop initiatives that provide a competitive edge in the talent market.

HR can gather competitive intelligence through various means, such as industry conferences, professional associations, and networking events. Engaging with former employees who have worked at competitor firms can also provide valuable insights. Additionally, HR should monitor public sources of information, such as company websites, press releases, and social media, to stay informed about competitor activities. This competitive intelligence can inform HR strategies in areas such as compensation, benefits, talent development, and organizational culture. By leveraging this knowledge, HR can position the organization as an employer of choice and attract top talent.

4. Managing Change and Organizational Adaptability

Sun Tzu's principle of using spies to gather foreknowledge before making strategic moves is crucial for HR's role in managing change and enhancing organizational adaptability. Effective change management requires a deep understanding of the organization's current state and potential obstacles.

HR should conduct thorough assessments before implementing major changes, such as restructuring, new technology adoption, or shifts in strategic direction. This involves gathering input from employees at all levels, as well as understanding external factors that may impact the organization. HR can use focus groups, pilot programs, and feedback loops to test new initiatives and gather data on their effectiveness. By collecting and analyzing this information, HR can make informed decisions that minimize disruption and enhance the organization's ability to adapt to change. This proactive approach ensures that the organization remains agile and responsive to evolving business environments.

5. Enhancing Employee Well-being and Engagement

Sun Tzu's focus on the importance of maintaining intimate relations with spies and rewarding them liberally can be translated to HR's efforts in enhancing employee well-being and engagement. Just as spies are vital for gathering crucial information, engaged and well-supported employees are essential for organizational success.

HR should prioritize initiatives that promote employee well-being, such as wellness programs, mental health resources, and flexible work arrangements. Regular recognition and reward programs can also boost morale and motivation. By actively listening to employees and addressing their needs, HR can create a supportive work environment that fosters loyalty and high performance. Furthermore, maintaining confidentiality and trust in HR practices ensures that employees feel safe and valued, encouraging open communication and engagement. This approach aligns with Sun Tzu's emphasis on treating spies with the utmost liberality and maintaining their trust.

6. Succession Planning

Sun Tzu's use of spies to gain foreknowledge and plan strategically can be directly applied to HR's succession planning efforts. Just as foreknowledge enables a general to anticipate and prepare for future battles, effective succession planning allows organizations to identify and develop future leaders, ensuring continuity and stability.

HR should implement a comprehensive succession planning process that identifies high-potential employees and provides them with targeted development opportunities. This can involve mentorship programs, leadership training, and rotational assignments that expose potential leaders to various aspects of the business. Additionally, HR should maintain a talent pipeline by regularly assessing and updating succession plans based on organizational needs and changes in the business environment. By preparing for future leadership transitions, HR can ensure that the organization remains resilient and capable of sustaining long-term success. This proactive approach to succession planning reflects Sun Tzu's strategy of using foreknowledge to achieve great results.

By applying Sun Tzu's principles of strategic intelligence and information management, HR can enhance its ability to gather critical insights, communicate effectively, manage change, foster employee well-being, and plan for future leadership transitions. These practices ultimately contribute to the organization's resilience and long-term success in a competitive business environment.

VII. Conclusion

Sun Tzu's principles of the use of spies offer valuable insights for HR professionals seeking to optimize their strategies and operations. By understanding and leveraging different sources of information, managing risks, and fostering a culture of trust and confidentiality, HR can enhance organizational resilience and performance. Effective HR management involves balancing proactive and reactive strategies, leveraging technology, and prioritizing continuous improvement. By applying these principles, HR can navigate the complexities of the modern workforce and drive organizational success.

In conclusion, Sun Tzu's principles provide a timeless framework for HR professionals to enhance their strategic capabilities. By anticipating challenges, leveraging strengths, and remaining adaptable, HR can create a dynamic and responsive work environment. This strategic approach ensures that the organization is well-prepared to meet future demands and achieve long-term success.

CONCLUSION: THE ART OF WAR'S IMPLICATIONS FOR HR

Sun Tzu's "The Art of War" offers timeless wisdom that can transform HR practices. The principles of strategic planning, adaptability, and effective leadership are as relevant today as they were over two millennia ago. By integrating these strategies into HR, organizations can navigate the complexities of modern business environments, achieve competitive advantages, and foster a resilient workforce.

Strategic Planning and Organizational Culture

One of the core lessons from "The Art of War" is the importance of strategic planning. For HR, this means developing clear, long-term plans that align with the company's goals and values. Ensuring that employees understand and share the organization's values (Moral Law) creates a cohesive and motivated workforce. A strong organizational culture reduces turnover, enhances performance, and builds loyalty.

Adapting to External and Internal Environments

Sun Tzu emphasizes understanding both the external environment (Heaven) and the internal environment (Earth). HR must stay informed about market conditions, economic cycles, and technological advancements to remain competitive.

This involves developing strategies that can quickly adapt to external changes. Internally, HR needs to leverage data to assess risks and opportunities, ensuring efficient resource allocation and operational effectiveness.

Effective Leadership

The Commander in Sun Tzu's framework represents leadership qualities such as wisdom, sincerity, benevolence, courage, and discipline. HR plays a crucial role in identifying, developing, and supporting leaders who embody these virtues. Effective leadership is essential for guiding and motivating employees, driving organizational success, and fostering a positive workplace culture.

Processes and Systems

Method and Discipline in "The Art of War" relate to establishing clear procedures and workflows. HR must implement efficient processes for recruitment, performance management, and employee engagement. Structured processes ensure that HR operations run smoothly and support the organization's strategic objectives. This includes maintaining efficient communication, managing resources effectively, and monitoring performance.

Flexibility and Adaptation

HR strategies must be flexible to respond to changing conditions. Sun Tzu's advice on adapting plans based on circumstances is crucial for HR professionals. Regularly reviewing and adjusting plans helps HR leverage favorable situations and address challenges. This adaptability is key to managing uncertainties and maintaining a strategic advantage.

Preparation and Calculations

Thorough planning and forecasting are critical in HR strategy. By calculating risks and potential outcomes, HR can make informed decisions that drive organizational success. Detailed plans provide a roadmap for achieving strategic goals and navigating challenges. Learning from past initiatives helps HR identify what works and what doesn't, promoting continuous improvement.

Practical Applications in HR

1. Talent Acquisition:

Effective talent acquisition aligns recruitment strategies with the company's values, ensuring a cultural fit that enhances employee engagement. HR must adapt recruitment tactics to changing market conditions and workforce trends, leveraging internal data to identify talent gaps and opportunities. Training and developing leadership within the HR team is crucial for building a strong HR function that can support organizational growth. Streamlining recruitment processes using efficient systems ensures timely and effective hiring decisions.

2. Employee Engagement and Retention:

Fostering a positive and cohesive workplace culture is vital for employee satisfaction and loyalty. Engagement strategies should be flexible to meet diverse employee needs and adapt to external factors. Regular assessment of internal factors such as team dynamics and work environment helps enhance the overall work atmosphere. Leadership programs that focus on motivating and retaining employees are essential for sustaining high levels of engagement. Clear communication channels and feedback systems are necessary to maintain a supportive and responsive work environment.

3. Performance Management:

Setting performance expectations that align with organizational goals ensures that employees' efforts contribute to the company's strategic objectives. Performance management practices must be adaptable to evolving business conditions, incorporating both qualitative and quantitative metrics. Regular monitoring of performance data helps identify strengths and areas for improvement, guiding interventions.

Providing leaders with the tools and training to manage and motivate their teams effectively is essential for achieving high performance. Structured performance review processes and fair reward systems recognize and incentivize employee contributions.

4. Learning and Development:

Aligning learning and development programs with organizational values and strategic goals promotes a culture of continuous improvement. Training programs should be updated to reflect current industry trends and technological advancements, ensuring employees have the skills needed for future challenges. Identifying internal skills gaps and development opportunities through assessments and feedback helps target learning initiatives effectively. Involving leaders in mentoring and developing their teams fosters a supportive learning environment. Clear training programs and career development paths provide employees with opportunities for growth and advancement.

5. Change Management:

Effective change management involves clearly communicating the importance of change initiatives to gain employee buy-in. HR must prepare for external changes and uncertainties that may impact the organization, developing strategies to manage them. Assessing the organization's readiness for change and identifying potential obstacles ensures smoother transitions. Leading change initiatives with a clear vision and strong leadership helps guide employees through the process. Implementing frameworks to manage and sustain change ensures that initiatives are successfully integrated into the organization.

6. Benefits, Total Rewards, and Compensation:

A comprehensive benefits and compensation strategy is essential for attracting and retaining top talent. HR must design competitive compensation packages that align with industry standards and organizational goals. Total rewards programs, which include bonuses, incentives, and non-monetary benefits, can enhance employee satisfaction and motivation. Regularly reviewing and adjusting these packages ensures they remain attractive and competitive. Transparent communication about benefits and rewards helps employees understand and appreciate their total compensation.

7. Leadership Development:

Investing in leadership development is crucial for creating a pipeline of future leaders. HR should design programs that identify high-potential employees and provide them with the skills and experiences needed for leadership roles. This includes mentorship, coaching, and leadership training. Effective leadership development programs align with the organization's strategic goals and prepare leaders to navigate future challenges. Ongoing support and development opportunities help retain top talent and ensure organizational continuity.

8. Corporate Culture:

Building and maintaining a strong corporate culture is vital for organizational success. HR plays a key role in defining and promoting the company's values, vision, and mission. Initiatives that celebrate diversity, inclusion, and collaboration contribute to a positive culture. Regularly assessing and nurturing the corporate culture ensures it evolves in line with organizational goals and employee expectations. A strong corporate culture fosters employee engagement, satisfaction, and loyalty.

9. Workforce Management:

Effective workforce management involves optimizing the use of human resources to meet organizational goals. HR must develop strategies for workforce planning, talent management, and succession planning. This includes identifying current and future workforce needs, managing talent pipelines, and ensuring the right people are in the right roles.

Workforce management also involves addressing issues such as absenteeism, turnover, and productivity. Strategic workforce management ensures the organization can meet its goals efficiently and effectively.

10. People Operations:

People operations encompass the administrative and operational aspects of HR, including payroll, compliance, and employee services. Streamlining these processes through technology and efficient systems enhances HR's ability to focus on strategic initiatives. Ensuring compliance with labor laws and regulations minimizes legal risks and promotes fair employment practices. Providing excellent employee services, such as onboarding and offboarding, enhances the overall employee experience and supports retention efforts.

11. HR Information Systems (HRIS):

Implementing and optimizing HRIS is crucial for managing HR processes and data efficiently. HRIS platforms can automate administrative tasks, track employee information, and provide data for decision-making. Effective use of HRIS improves accuracy, reduces administrative burden, and enhances HR's strategic capabilities. Regularly updating and integrating HRIS with other organizational systems ensures seamless operations and data flow. Training HR staff to effectively use HRIS maximizes its benefits and supports organizational goals.

12. Employee and Labor Relations:

Maintaining positive employee and labor relations is essential for a harmonious workplace. HR must develop policies and practices that promote fair treatment, open communication, and conflict resolution. Engaging with labor unions and negotiating collective bargaining agreements requires strategic planning and negotiation skills. Addressing employee grievances promptly and effectively helps maintain trust and morale. Positive employee and labor relations contribute to a stable and productive work environment.

Future Trends and Considerations

1. Technological Advancements:

AI and automation are transforming HR practices, offering tools that streamline recruitment, automate performance management, and personalize learning experiences. Preparing for the future of work involves integrating these technologies effectively to remain adaptive and competitive. AI-powered tools can enhance efficiency by automating routine tasks and providing data-driven insights for decision-making. Embracing technological advancements enables HR to focus on strategic activities that drive organizational success.

2. Globalization and Diversity:

Managing a diverse and global workforce requires adapting HR strategies to different cultural and regulatory environments. Embracing diversity and inclusion enhances organizational innovation and performance. HR professionals must develop cultural competence to manage diverse teams effectively, ensuring compliance with various labor laws and regulations. Inclusive policies and practices promote a supportive environment where all employees feel valued and respected, driving engagement and productivity.

3. Sustainability and Corporate Social Responsibility:

Integrating sustainability into HR strategies promotes ethical practices and social responsibility. Green HR practices and initiatives that support environmental sustainability align with broader organizational goals. HR can lead efforts in corporate social responsibility, ensuring that the organization operates ethically and sustainably. By promoting sustainability, HR helps build a positive corporate reputation and meets the expectations of stakeholders who prioritize environmental and social governance.

4. Employee Well-being and Mental Health:

Prioritizing employee well-being and mental health is

increasingly important in today's workplace. HR must develop programs that support physical, mental, and emotional health, creating a balanced work environment. Initiatives such as wellness programs, flexible working arrangements, and mental health resources help employees manage stress and maintain a healthy work-life balance. Fostering a culture that values well-being enhances overall productivity and reduces absenteeism.

5. Workforce Analytics and AI:

Leveraging AI-driven workforce analytics allows HR to make data-driven decisions that improve organizational performance. AI can analyze vast amounts of data on employee turnover, engagement, performance, and other key metrics to identify trends and inform strategic initiatives. By employing machine learning algorithms, AI can provide predictive insights that help HR anticipate future challenges and opportunities. These AI-driven analytics optimize talent management, enhance employee experience, and support strategic planning. By embracing AI-powered data-driven approaches, HR can better align its strategies with organizational goals and drive success.

Sun Tzu's "The Art of War" provides a strategic framework that HR professionals can use to navigate modern organizational challenges. By applying these timeless principles, HR can build resilient, adaptable, and successful organizations.

THE ART OF WAR

Strategic HR Applications for Today's Workforce

EPILOGUE

As we draw the curtain on this exploration of Sun Tzu's "The Art of War" and its profound implications for HR, it is evident that the ancient wisdom encapsulated in this timeless classic holds invaluable lessons for modern organizational leadership and human resources management. The journey through the strategies and philosophies of Sun Tzu has illuminated the parallels between the battlefield and the corporate world, offering a unique perspective on how HR leaders can navigate the complexities of today's business environment with strategic acumen and foresight.

The principles outlined in "The Art of War" provide a robust framework for HR professionals to build and execute effective strategies that drive organizational success. From the foundational concept of "Laying Plans" to the intricate tactics of "Maneuvering" and "Energy," each chapter of Sun Tzu's work has been meticulously interpreted to align with contemporary HR practices. This epilogue aims to encapsulate the key insights gained from this exploration and reinforce the enduring relevance of Sun Tzu's teachings in the realm of human resources.

The Strategic Role of HR

The role of HR has evolved significantly over the years, transitioning from a primarily administrative function to a strategic partner in organizational success. Sun Tzu's emphasis on strategic planning, understanding the environment, and leveraging internal strengths resonates deeply with the modern

HR mandate. HR leaders today are tasked with not only managing talent but also driving cultural transformation, fostering innovation, and ensuring organizational resilience.

By adopting a strategic mindset akin to that of a battlefield general, HR professionals can anticipate challenges, devise effective responses, and create a work environment that promotes engagement, productivity, and loyalty. The principles of "The Art of War" serve as a guide for HR leaders to think strategically, act decisively, and lead with vision and purpose.

Adapting to Change and Uncertainty

One of the most valuable lessons from Sun Tzu is the importance of adaptability and flexibility in the face of change. The business landscape is constantly evolving, influenced by technological advancements, economic fluctuations, and shifting workforce dynamics. HR leaders must be adept at navigating these changes, much like a general maneuvering through varied terrains and unpredictable conditions.

The ability to adapt plans based on changing circumstances, as emphasized in the chapters on "Variation of Tactics" and "Weak Points and Strong," is crucial for HR success. This involves staying informed about industry trends, anticipating potential disruptions, and being prepared to pivot strategies as needed. By fostering a culture of agility and continuous improvement, HR can ensure that the organization remains competitive and resilient in a dynamic environment.

The Power of Leadership

Leadership is a central theme in both Sun Tzu's teachings and effective HR management. The qualities of a good leader —wisdom, sincerity, courage, and discipline—are as relevant today as they were in ancient times. HR leaders play a pivotal role in identifying, developing, and nurturing leadership talent within the organization. By doing so, they ensure that the organization is equipped with leaders who can inspire, motivate, and guide their teams toward achieving strategic objectives.

Sun Tzu's insights on leadership, particularly the importance of leading by example and maintaining discipline, provide valuable guidance for HR professionals. Effective leadership development programs, mentoring initiatives, and a strong focus on ethical leadership can significantly enhance organizational performance and employee satisfaction.

Building a Strong Organizational Culture

The concept of the "Moral Law," which emphasizes unity and loyalty, underscores the importance of a strong organizational culture. A positive and cohesive culture is the bedrock of employee engagement, retention, and overall organizational success. HR leaders are the custodians of culture, responsible for fostering an environment that aligns with the organization's values and mission.

By embedding the principles of respect, integrity, and collaboration into the fabric of the organization, HR can create a workplace where employees feel valued and motivated. This, in turn, drives higher levels of performance and innovation, contributing to the long-term success of the organization.

Strategic Talent Management

Talent management is a critical aspect of HR strategy, encompassing recruitment, development, and retention. Sun Tzu's emphasis on understanding the strengths and weaknesses of both one's own forces and the enemy provides valuable insights for talent management. By leveraging data and analytics, HR can gain a deeper understanding of the workforce, identify skill gaps, and develop targeted strategies to attract, develop, and retain top talent.

Effective talent management involves creating a compelling employer brand, offering opportunities for continuous learning and growth, and implementing fair and transparent performance management systems. By aligning talent management strategies with organizational goals, HR can ensure that the organization has the right people in the right roles, driving success and competitive advantage.

Conclusion: A Timeless Guide for Modern HR

In conclusion, the teachings of Sun Tzu in "The Art of War" offer a timeless guide for modern HR professionals. The strategic principles and insights provided in this classic work are as relevant today as they were centuries ago, offering a powerful framework for navigating the complexities of human resources management. By embracing these principles, HR leaders can enhance their strategic capabilities, foster a positive and resilient organizational culture, and drive sustainable success.

As we look to the future, the integration of Sun Tzu's wisdom with contemporary HR practices will continue to provide valuable guidance for HR professionals seeking to excel in their roles and make a meaningful impact on their organizations. The journey through "The Art of War" for HR has been an enlightening and inspiring exploration, reinforcing the importance of strategic thinking, adaptability, and strong leadership in the ever-changing field of human resources.

If you have enjoyed this book, please provide a rating and review on Amazon.

ABOUT THE AUTHOR

Tim Glowa

Tim Glowa, an accomplished consultant, stands out as an authority in Human Capital Strategy, ESG, and AI-driven HR solutions. He founded HR Brain, an AI startup transforming HR practices by addressing diversity biases, assessing corporate culture, and predicting employee churn using advanced AI technologies. Glowa's career, marked by significant roles at Grant Thornton and Ernst & Young, reflects his commitment to driving fact-based decisions in human capital and ESG spaces. His work has guided global organizations in attracting, retaining, and rewarding employees, demonstrating a deep understanding of the evolving challenges in the corporate world.

A thought leader frequently cited in prestigious outlets like the Wall Street Journal, Forbes, and Barron's, Glowa's insights into human capital strategies are widely respected. His contributions to Directorship Magazine and conferences with the National Association of Corporate Directors (NACD) highlight his dedication to educating board members, especially independent directors, about the importance of effective governance in AI and human capital management. Holding both an International Board Director Competency Designation (IBDC.D) and a Global ESG Board Certification, his expertise spans across various industry verticals, making him a valuable asset to any board or organization.

Tim Glowa's unique blend of entrepreneurial spirit, expertise in AI and HR, and commitment to responsible governance positions him as a sought-after advisor and potential board member. At HRbrain, he leverages AI to revolutionize HR practices, from mitigating diversity biases to enhancing employee engagement and development. Available for consulting on AI and human capital challenges and selective board roles, Glowa continues to influence the corporate governance landscape, advocating for strategic and ethical AI integration and human capital management in today's fast-paced business environment.

He is the author of the book "Smart Board Governance for the AI Revolution".

BOOKS BY THIS AUTHOR

The Art Of War

The Art of War by Sun Tzu is a timeless treatise on military strategy and tactics, revered for its profound insights that extend beyond the battlefield to modern realms like business, leadership, and human resources. Composed over 2,500 years ago, this classic text delves into the essence of conflict, offering wisdom on how to approach and manage disputes, strategize for victory, and ultimately secure success through intelligent planning and adaptability.

Sun Tzu emphasizes the importance of understanding both oneself and the enemy, advocating for thorough preparation and flexibility in the face of changing circumstances. He explores various elements of warfare, such as the significance of terrain, the use of spies, and the value of deception. His teachings stress that the acme of skill lies not in winning battles but in subduing the enemy without fighting, highlighting the power of strategy over brute force.

In the corporate world, The Art of War serves as a manual for navigating competitive landscapes, fostering innovation, and cultivating leadership. Its principles guide leaders to make calculated decisions, anticipate challenges, and leverage strengths while minimizing weaknesses. The text's insights into team dynamics, resource allocation, and strategic thinking are as relevant today as they were in ancient China.

This timeless wisdom is not just for military enthusiasts or historians; it offers valuable lessons for anyone looking to excel in their field. Whether you are leading a company, managing a team, or striving for personal excellence, The Art of War provides a strategic framework to achieve your goals with precision and efficiency. This enduring classic is a must-read for anyone seeking to master the art of strategic thinking and outmaneuver their competition.

This contains the original text of Sun Tzu's book, a translation by Lionel Giles, with an introduction by Tim Glowa

Smart Board Governance For The Ai Revolution

"Smart Board Governance for the Artificial Intelligence Revolution" by Tim Glowa offers an essential guide for independent directors, emphasizing their crucial role in governance as it pertains to AI, rather than the execution of AI strategies. Glowa argues that in the rapidly advancing AI revolution, boards must be well-versed in AI to effectively oversee and govern its integration in corporate strategies. The book underscores the need for a paradigm shift in boardrooms, advocating for enhanced AI literacy among directors to ensure ethical, strategic, and effective AI oversight, aligning with corporate values and governance principles.

Glowa highlights the transformative impact of AI on industries and business operations, stressing the importance of board-level oversight in navigating these changes responsibly. The book delves into various case studies from Fortune 1000 companies, illustrating the complexities and practical considerations of AI governance. Glowa's narrative is a call to action for board members to embrace continuous learning and adaptation, focusing on the pivotal role of AI in reshaping corporate governance and strategy.

In conclusion, "Smart Board Governance for the AI Revolution" serves as a comprehensive resource for board members to understand and oversee AI's integration into business models and operations. The book advocates for a proactive approach, equipping board members with the knowledge and tools necessary for responsible AI governance, ultimately steering organizations towards sustainable and ethical AI utilization in the business world.

Employee Preference Optimization: A Strategic Guide

"Employee Preference Optimization" is a comprehensive guide on aligning total rewards with employee preferences to enhance satisfaction and drive organizational success. Authored by Tim Glowa, the book draws on his extensive experience in human capital analytics, emphasizing the importance of data-driven decision-making in employee benefits optimization. It introduces the concept of Employee Preference Optimization (EPO) and details a five-stage process for effectively implementing EPO, from understanding employee needs to evaluating the success of reward programs. The book also highlights the role of conjoint analysis in understanding employee preferences, making it a crucial tool for HR professionals. Overall, it provides strategic insights into creating a more fulfilling and productive work environment through tailored employee benefits.

www.ingramcontent.com/pod-product-compliance
Lightning Source LLC
Chambersburg PA
CBHW071452220526
45472CB00003B/765